40¢
55

This book may be kept

FOURTEEN DAYS

A fine will be charged for each day the book is kept overtime.

GAYLORD 142

Unfinished Business

UNFINISHED BUSINESS

Short Diversions on Religious Themes

by HALFORD E. LUCCOCK

HARPER & BROTHERS · PUBLISHERS · NEW YORK

✿ Contents

	Overture	9
1.	*Unfinished Business*	13
2.	*Meeting Yourself at Age Forty*	15
3.	*"What a Cast!"*	17
4.	*Nevertheless*	18
5.	*"Show Me First Your Penny"*	19
6.	*"When the Brain Muscles In"*	21
7.	*God Asks Some Questions*	23
8.	*"Casting Problems Are Holding Up Production"*	25
9.	*Famous Last Words*	26
10.	*A Date with the Gulf Stream*	28
11.	*Life Begins at Forty*	30
12.	*"Shrink or Expand"*	31
13.	*What Is It All About?*	32
14.	*Keeping Six Clocks Ticking Together*	33
15.	*"Thou Shouldst be Living at This Hour"*	35
16.	*Molehills Out of Mountains*	37
17.	*Danger Ahead—Marriage!*	39
18.	*Image Making and Breaking*	41
19.	*Tolerance or Rubber Spine?*	43
20.	*Handshakes Across the Years*	44
21.	*The Age of Collecting*	46
22.	*Zigzagging Through Life*	48
23.	*"Dead Money"*	50
24.	*"How Do You Play It?"*	52

6   *Contents*

25. "No Faith in the Future"   54
26. Outliving Yourself   56
27. False Promises   57
28. How Do You Talk to Yourself?   59
29. Living Upside Down   61
30. Minority Reports   62
31. "I'm All Alone"   64
32. A Human Chain   66
33. "Let the Rest of the World Go By"   68
34. "No Business that Required Entry"   69
35. "I Find No Fault"   71
36. "She Knew It"   72
37. Landscape and "Inscape"   73
38. "You Look Like a Million Dollars"   75
39. The 100 Most Important People   76
40. The Church Belongs to Me   78
41. 113 by 26   79
42. A Message from Mars   80
43. Penurious Living   82
44. A Knock at the Door   84
45. Is God on Your Christmas List?   86
46. The Rescue of Jesus   87
47. In Debt to Palestine   89
48. Cut Off from the Past   91
49. The Royal Road to Romance   92
50. Something for Nothing   94
51. Deficiency Diseases   96
52. Look!   98
53. Stalemate   100

54. "I Saw Also *the* Lord"   102
55. Three Classes of People   103
56. Adventures with Discarded Materials   104
57. Explorer   106
58. Dire Poverty   109
59. Noise and Fog   111
60. "For an Easier Key"   113
61. Anybody's Guess   115
62. The Baby Grew Up   116
63. "You Can't Prove It by Me"   117
64. Incentives for Living   119
65. Your View of the World   121
66. Running Away from Life   123
67. The Devil's Creed   125
68. The Stubs of an Old Checkbook   127
69. "The Airy Grace of a Country Club"   128
70. Natural History of Nonsense   130
71. Bang and Whimper   132
72. "The Victim Suffered Consciousness"   133
73. Anonymous   135
74. What God Hath Put Asunder   137
75. "Casually Yours"   139
76. Saved by an Idea   140
77. Antiquated Geography   141
78. A "Vulnerable Heart"   143
79. "Jesus Himself Drew Near"   145
80. Are You a Fanatic?   147
81. The Grumbler   149
82. Two Kinds of Prayer   150

8   *Contents*

83. *Missing the Cue*   *151*
84. *Playing for Safety*   *152*
85. *Summoning the Devil*   *153*
86. *Hideout*   *155*
87. *How Not to Pray*   *157*
88. *"A Company on a Side Street"*   *158*
89. *Imagine That!*   *160*
90. *A World Gone Sane*   *162*
91. *Growing Up to Maturity*   *164*
92. *When You Can't Do Anything*   *166*
93. *Find Yourself in This Picture*   *167*
94. *"Like Something Was Going to Happen"*   *168*
95. *Is Jesus a "Back Number"?*   *169*
96. *Going to the Dogs*   *171*
97. *The Embarrassment of Ancestors*   *172*
98. *"This Little Pig Went to Market"*   *174*
99. *How Irritable Are You?*   *176*
100. *"I Want to Be a Christian—in My Head"*   *178*
101. *The Saints Preserve Us!*   *180*
102. *"So Easily Beset Us"*   *182*
103. *The Zero Hour*   *184*
104. *Challenging an Axiom*   *185*
105. *Accessories Before the Fact*   *187*
106. *Extraordinary!*   *189*
107. *"I Need the Church When . . ."*   *191*

✿ Overture

ALL THE short pieces in this volume are bits of *Unfinished Business*. They start, but they do not finish. They do not aspire to be more than starting points for thought. The hope has been that they may at least disclose some beckoning roads which may allure the reader to follow.

These points of departure are called "Diversions." A diversion, the dictionary confides, is something that does not have the solemn determination of a bulldozer, or the steady whack of a pile driver. It is much less grim and more festive. It is more like a few rhythmic steps on a village green.

Grateful acknowledgment is made to the editors of *The Chaplain* and *Pulpit Digest* for permission to include some material which appeared in those periodicals.

HALFORD E. LUCCOCK

New Haven, Connecticut

Unfinished Business

1 ✸ Unfinished Business

"IS THERE any Unfinished Business?"

The chairman raps for order, calling for what is usually the first item on the agenda, following the reading of the minutes. The members of the meeting try to rub the cobwebs out of their memories and recall what was left unfinished at the last meeting.

"Unfinished Business" is the first item on the world's agenda. The whole story of the world, and of man on earth, is the exciting tale of catching up with unfinished business. All the sciences, biology, geology, zoology, paleontology, psychology, and also history, philosophy, religion, and law, have added their chapters. It is a continued story, a thriller, and often a "shocker," the top mystery story, which has been unfolding for millions of years. We are born into the midst of it.

In his fascinating book, *Conversation with the Earth*, Hans Clous, the geologist has a vivid word on this unfinished business. He writes, "I knew geology at second hand from books, but at the age of twenty-four, I became a geologist forever by seeing with my own eyes Vesuvius in eruption. I cried, 'The earth is alive!' The earth—the permanent and time-honored stage of our growing, being and dying, thunders and bursts and throws acrid fumes into the pure air that we breathe." The world was not petrified, but is living!

From the viewpoint of Christian faith the exhilarating sense of incompleteness, of the dynamic, rather than the static quality of the universe, is memorably expressed in William DeWitt Hyde's hymn,

> Creation's Lord, we give Thee thanks
> That this, Thy world is incomplete;
> That battle calls our marshalled ranks;
> That work awaits our hands and feet.

Our world is not chaos; it is work in progress.

The basic truth, of course, is that man himself is unfinished busi-

13

ness. Christopher Morley defines man as a "folder of unfinished business," a truly scientific description! For it is true biologically and historically. The physical man, his body and his brain, were unfinished business for millions of years. Scientists tell us that man's body is still unfinished. They find that man's stature has been growing in the past two centuries, if we average all men together. The span of life is growing longer. Margaret Mead, the distinguished anthropologist, has a striking phrase to picture the later progress of man. The drama of evolution is that of "half-brained men becoming men." It is a delusion that man is static. As another anthropologist reports, "Man is unbelievably malleable." Yet people talk in an ignorant way as though man were as finished as an ax from the stone age. They babble the old cliché, like a parrot crying "Polly wants a cracker," that "you can't change human nature." As though human nature were something set in concrete! Sir Norman Angell makes the effective answer, "We cannot change human nature, but we can change belief and behavior." And that is what is needed.

Each person is "unfinished business." It does not yet appear what we shall be. It is a great mistake to close the books before the day is done.

The world of nations is still an unfinished symphony. That is the name of the major work of Schubert's Symphony in B Minor, which was written in 1822 and left unpublished, finally to be brought out and called "The Unfinished Symphony." That name symbolizes the possibility of mankind—harmony. Not like the old so-called "Concert of Europe," in which the bass of the heavy artillery drowned out all music but its own.

The far reach of faith is found in other lines of the hymn quoted:

> That Thou hast not yet finished man,
> That we are in the making still,
> As friends who share the Maker's plan,
> As sons who know the Father's will.

2 ❈ *Meeting Yourself at Age Forty*

A N ENGLISHMAN, Osbert Sitwell, once wrote a novel that had a memorable scene in it, even though it was only fancy. The novel was entitled *The Man Who Lost Himself*. In the middle of it there was a scene where the hero was trailing a person in Paris. He wanted to know if the man he was after was stopping at a certain hotel. He figured out that one way to do it without exciting suspicion would be to go to the clerk and ask him if he himself— giving his own name—was registered there. Then, when the clerk was looking at the register, he could glance down the page and see if the name of the other man was entered.

So he carried out the plan and then got the shock of his life! The clerk looked up and said: "Yes, he has been waiting for you. He is in Room 40. I will have you shown right up." There was nothing to do but go through with it, so the man followed the bell boy to Room 40. And it is there that the story goes off the deep end. For when he went into the room, there he found a man remarkably like himself— a little more gray, a little more heavy, but undeniably himself. The person he met was himself as he would be at the age of forty, just twenty years ahead.

It was all a fancy, of course; but it has this truth: there is a man out there in the future waiting for each of us, the man we will be twenty years ahead. Suppose you are in your early twenties. Out ahead of you is the man you will be at forty-two or forty-four. How will you like him?

There is only one real way that one can get any line on the kind of man he will be. Of course, we can do a lot of guessing, or "wishful thinking." We might want him to be rich or famous. But the only true line we can get on him is by projecting as in an architect's drawing, the lines on which we are now going. Suppose you keep on for twenty years just as you are now. What kind of picture will you make? Are your present directions and habits good enough to keep up for twenty years?

15

If you do keep them up, will there be any chance of their resulting in a man you would be proud to meet? Run them out in your imagination and see what the prospects are. Have you got enough inner strength to pull through the tough going the years up to middle life will bring? Have you a big enough motive for living?

If you are not satisfied with the picture you see when you project your present conduct twenty years ahead, now is the time to change to other ways and other aims that will forecast a better future. Christian faith and discipleship will bring into life the lines of direction that lead into what Jesus called "abundant life."

3 ✶ "What a Cast!"

A PLAYWRIGHT in New York City, not long ago, was looking up a number in the New York Telephone Directory. As
he held the gigantic book in his hands, he thought of his
craft as a dramatist and said: "There is not much plot here, but boy,
what a cast!"

It is a great cast—pages and pages of Cohens, O'Briens, Smiths,
Joneses, and Robinsons. Just imagine what a World Directory would
be, with two billion names in it! A stunning cast—

> Rich man, poor man, beggar man, thief,
> Doctor, lawyer, merchant, chief.

All races, religions, occupations, colors, classes, all in the cast!

Now if we could only give that cast a plot, the making of community—what a drama it would be!

That, in an unusual picture, is the enterprise of the Kingdom of
God, to bring into the life of the people of the earth, that cast with
staggering dramatic possibilities, a divine plot, a family drama, in
which the sons and daughters of God live and work together!

That same need often appears in an individual life also. Here are a
group of people of great potentialities, who have no *plot* to their
lives. The busy little anecdotes in which they engage themselves do
not add up to any great purpose and enterprise. Christian discipleship, however, brings an exciting plot into a life or a group of lives.

The same need appears at times in a church. The members make
a great cast, a *dramatis personnae* of unmeasured capacities but they
often lack a commanding plot; they have not given themselves whole-
heartedly and unitedly to the superb plot of making Jesus Christ
known, loved, and obeyed in their community and throughout the
world.

17

4 ❖ *Nevertheless*

WHEN HENRIK IBSEN, the Norwegian dramatist, came to die, his last word was "Nevertheless." He was a great critic of the society in which he lived, a great objector and debater. It was fitting that this should be his last word. Just as he started to say something in rebuttal to what had been said, he got out the word, "Nevertheless," and then death struck suddenly.

A good word for the last word, "Nevertheless." In a very real way that is what Christian faith is all about. It takes an honest look at all the evil in the world. It faces all of life's confusions, its frustrations, its suffering, its disaster, and says: "Nevertheless." It was true in the very beginning of Christian history. In the Crucifixion of Jesus, all the agents of evil had done their utmost: Judas, Caiaphas, Pilate, and the mob. "Nevertheless," on the first day of the week, "as it began to dawn . . ." There is a beautiful picture of that in an Edinburgh cemetery, at the grave of the little daughter of Sir James Simpson, the discoverer of chloroform. On her tombstone are carved her name and the words: "Nevertheless I Live."

We find the word used in a connection similar to the plight of our world today, the feeling that disaster was imminent. We read in II Peter 3:10: "The heavens will pass away with a loud noise, and the elements will be dissolved with fire, and the earth and the works that are upon it will be burned up." Doesn't that sound exactly like a description of the effect of a hydrogen bomb? Yet in the face of that we read on: *"Nevertheless* we look for a new heaven and a new earth." That was Christian faith in the first century. It must be our faith in the twentieth.

5 ❋ "Show Me First Your Penny"

EVERY READER has already recognized the line quoted above as coming from that truly great work of philosophy and English history, *Mother Goose*. Anyone who thinks that *Mother Goose* is just a child's book is greatly mistaken. It is no more merely a child's book than is *Aesop's Fables* or *Gulliver's Travels*. It is worth noting that no book has ever become an accepted child's classic which was not primarily a book for adults. In *Mother Goose* there are many profound observations and echoes of social history.

Consider Simple Simon:

> Simple Simon met a pieman
> Going to the fair.
> Said Simple Simon to the pieman,
> "Let me taste your ware."
> Said the pieman to Simple Simon,
> "Show me first your penny."

That was the catch—the penny.

We all begin life as Simple Simons getting our first look at the world's bewildering fair. There are so many things that are entrancing that we say excitedly: "I'd like some of that. Let me taste your ware." Then we are confronted with life's inexorable demand for a down payment—"first your penny."

It is true of a marriage. A lifelong happy marriage is a shining prize. But there is a down payment needed, not the payment on a washing machine or a refrigerator, though that may be hard enough. What is demanded is the great down payment—discipline, the subjection of self, patience, love "to the level of every day's most quiet need."

It is true in the realm of religion. Take prayer, for instance. People have seen that prayer has often been a real power in the lives of

19

persons they have known. They would like to have that power. They do not realize the cost. They must first show their earnest and sustained desire for such spiritual reserve power. They must "show their penny" in the form of establishing a habit of prayer. There is need for a life in harmony with God, so that prayer is a real communion with God, and not a mass of words; the need to ask in the spirit of Jesus, and not just send orders to God, demanding, "Give me, give me, give me."

The same is true of influencing people for good. In our highest moments we all want "some of that." We say eagerly to life, "Let me taste that ware." But there is first the necessity of showing our penny of determination. To be really helpful to people demands a self-forgetfulness, a willingness to spend and be spent, to lose our life and find it in the larger life of others. That is a high cost.

So also in the life of a church. It is easy to pray, "O God, bless our church and make it great." That is a noble prayer, but it is also a dangerous one. There is only one way for a church to be really great, and that is the way that Jesus pointed out, "If any of you would be great, let him be a servant." That is the price of greatness, the only greatness there is in the Christian sense. A church, small or large, can have that greatness, if it is willing to pay the price.

6 ❖ "When the Brain Muscles In"

T HE PHRASE above comes from Edward K. Smith's book of some years ago, *Last Train from Berlin*. He is describing the stunning spectacle which Hitler used to stage in the nineteen thirties at Nuremburg, Germany, with the enormous parade of the growing war machine. He says that his eye was caught and his nerve stirred by the magnificence of the spectacle, the marching columns, the bands. It was a great show. Then, he said, after a while, "the brain muscles in" to this emotional excitement and he remembered the dire threat made to the world by all this might and power. He was struck with the thought that, when analyzed, this was a terribly obscene spectacle, after all.

A good phrase, that—"when the brain muscles in." It represents the means of salvation from many of the destructive forces of life. Think of how the brain muscled in on the emotional orgy that gave rise to dueling. It was made into a matter of honor, that when a man called you an ugly name you had to go out and shoot each other. Alexander Hamilton and Aaron Burr had a long rivalry. One called the other a liar, so they had to go out and shoot, and the young United States lost one of its great minds, Hamilton. Then, finally, the world's brain muscled in on that idiotic code, and abolished it. So with slavery. It was violently defended by men's traditions and emotions. They said the world has always had slavery and always would. Then after centuries, the brain muscled in; men began to think and showed up slavery as not only morally degrading but economically bad.

There is need for the brain muscling in on one's own life. Dissipation has a pull. "This is the life!" it cries. Let yourself go. Then is time for the brain to "muscle in," and let a person have a sharp glimpse of the end of the road; make him see the waste of opportunity and health and self-respect, that come from the "what-the-hell-let-

21

yourself-go" program. Give the brain, the clear-eyed reason, a chance
to take over the emotions.

There is also need for the brain to muscle in on social practices
such as war.

7 ✿ *God Asks Some Questions*

IN HIS play *An Inspector Calls*, J. B. Priestley portrays vividly how we belong to one another, though we easily miss the interrelatedness of life.

A police inspector calls upon a respectable middle-class family to ask some questions. A little girl, Eva Smith, has committed suicide. Does the respectable citizen know anything of her? He does not recall the name, but under questioning recalls that he sacked her from his factory because she wanted another half-dollar a week. What does the daughter know of her? Nothing, till shown the girl's photograph. Then she realizes that this was the shop assistant about whom she had complained in a fit of bad temper, and who had been dismissed in consequence. Each one around the prosperous merchant's table— his wife, his son, his prospective son-in-law, had helped to push Eva Smith into the darkness where she took her life.

The unique thing about this play develops as the play progresses, when the police inspector appears less and less like an officer of the law and more and more like God. The most searching third degree (if the phrase may be permitted in a most reverent use) through which any of us will ever be put will be the questionings of God. For God could go through any congregation on a Sunday morning and search those present to the marrow of their souls with questions about how they lived among their fellows. There would be questions about one's responsibility in the affairs of his time.

"Did you know the boys down the street who got into trouble with the law?"

"Well, not exactly. A few months ago the church tried to start a Scout Troup for this gang of boys, but I was too busy to bother with it."

"Did you know the colored family across the tracks whose boy has become a nuisance as a drunkard around town?"

"Yes, I knew them. The boy was an honor student in our high

23

school. After school he seemed to change a lot. No, we didn't give him a job in our office, because we only employ whites. I don't know whether he was allowed to join the beach club or go into the recreation center. I know he spent a lot of time with a no-good crowd in the tavern. Guess it was the only place he could go in town."

"Did you know anything about the Chinese children who suffered from tuberculosis in Hunan Province last year?"

"No. How would I know anything about that? All I know about that long-sounding name in China is what I heard about it in church a year ago. I didn't listen very carefully; something about a campaign to build a sanitarium out there. I just passed it off as another cry for money. Taxes were so high anyway, and I couldn't keep up my membership in the yacht club. Were those the children who were exposed to tuberculosis?"

And so the questions come, one after another. God asks them about our whole lives. As the questioning goes on, one fact emerges from all the admissions and denials—*we are members one of another*.

No man liveth or dieth unto himself. Each is responsible for all, and all are responsible for each one. A central theme will always be the question asked first by every chief inspector when the defendant takes the stand: "Where were you on the night when one of my children needed help?"

8 ✽ "Casting Problems Are Holding Up Production"

THE SENTENCE above is probably the one most frequently found in notices of forthcoming theatrical enterprises. Everything else is ready. The script of the play is done. The scenery has been designed and created. The financial backing has been secured. Then "casting problems" arise.

Who can play the part in a way that will make the whole thing live? It is easy enough for a college dramatic society, for instance, or a commercial theater, to say "Let's put on Hamlet." It is a great play. But who will play Hamlet? In Hamlet's own words: "Ay there's the rub." For the problems of casting a production, of finding the men and women able to enact the drama, are always the biggest ones.

That is the problem of Christianity in the world, the number one problem, beside which everything else is easy. The script is all ready. In the Gospel there is the great drama of redemption all written out, waiting for the right cast. The scenery is waiting, in the world, and in the physical equipment of the churches. But "casting problems are holding up production."

Often the living actors are missing, men and women who can give an adequately powerful demonstration of a Word. Here is a community, for instance, waiting for the production of the Christian drama of salvation for individual and society in Christ. But it does not arrive on the stage, for the people to create it are lacking.

Who can play the part of Peter, capable of impulsive, headlong devotion?

Who can play the necessary part of Andrew, who sought out new disciples of Jesus?

Who can play the part of multitudes of people unknown to fame, in whose lives Christ, lived, and who carried forward his designs in all parts of the earth?

25

9 ✿ *Famous Last Words*

THE CUSTOM of recording and remembering the last words of persons is not followed today as it was a generation or two ago. For one thing, most persons die quietly in their sleep and do not pronounce any last words consciously. But it is an interesting matter to recall some last words that have been recorded. Many of them show great courage and unshaken faith, unafraid of any amazement.

One notable last remark may not seem to display any pious mood, yet it is a word of high faith. That is the last sentence said by Professor Samuel F. Upham, a man of great learning, wit, and faith and for many years a teacher at Drew Theological Seminary. When the end was near, family and friends gathered at his bedside. Someone said that Dr. Upham was already dead. Another answered: "Feel his feet. No one ever died with warm feet." Then Dr. Upham opened an eye and said: "Joan of Arc did." Those were his last words. And they were really great ones. For the wit and humor persisting to the very end were the expression of a high faith without fear.

Some of the best-known last words are those of John Wesley: "The best of all is, God is with us." Oliver Cromwell, looking at the mournful faces around his deathbed, said: "Will no one here thank God?" Both are moving declarations of a faith that never wavered.

In our own day there is that beautiful last sentence said by Dr. Peter Marshall, the Washington minister. In his biography, *A Man Called Peter*, written by his wife, she records that as he was being carried out of his house on a stretcher on his way to the hospital he said to his wife, casually: "I'll see you in the morning." That night he died. But the words are a fine and true expression of Christian faith. This is what death means to a Christian: "I'll see you in the morning."

But sometimes the last words are neither noble nor words of faith.

Think of the last words of P. T. Barnum: "What were today's receipts?"

Here is one on a higher level, but not high enough. William Hazlitt, the nineteenth-century essayist, said as his exit line: "Well, I've had a happy life." That showed a large spirit, with no bitter complaint. But think more deeply. Frank Swinnerton says of this last word: "Which of us, uncertain travelers as we all are on uncharted ways, could ask or say more?" The answer to the question is that multitudes have asked and said a whole lot more. It is not enough to have had a happy life.

Similar to this is the last word of Lady Mary Wortley Montague, in the eighteenth century: "It has all been very interesting." What a summary of life—"interesting"!

Contrast with that, the word of Jesus on the cross: "It is finished." He had been given work to do by his Father, and he had accomplished it. The acceptance of a great commission from God lifts life out of triviality and selfishness.

The greatest of last words are those of Jesus: "Father, into thy hands I commit my spirit." Jesus said this at the end of his life. But he also said it at the beginning of his ministry at the temptation. They are words to say at the beginning and all the way through to the end.

10 ✿ A Date with the Gulf Stream

A FEW years ago a little ship put out from a port on the Gulf of Mexico, headed for a port on the northeastern coast of the United States. The ship was not only small and much the worse for wear; it looked like something left over from Admiral Farragut's attack on New Orleans in the Civil War. Quite a crowd of friends of the skipper, and a chorus who came to jeer, gathered for the embarkation. They had a lot of sport.

"You won't get anywhere in that tub," was the cheering send-off.

"Oh, yes, I will," confidently replied the skipper.

"What makes you think so?" he was asked by many of the bystanders.

"I've got a date," he replied. "I've got a date with the Gulf Stream." And he had!

The skipper was a mariner, first class. He knew his winds and water. He had a definite date with a power greater than himself or his little craft. He was not sailing under his own wit or the momentum of his engines alone. He had a date with a power not of himself that made for marine "righteousness."

The fortification the skipper found in the confidence in his "date with the Gulf Stream" comes, I think, close to the experience of every one of us. It is certainly true, is it not, that our first and deepest need is for the renewal of the sense that, however uncharted the sea or land on which we travel, we have a date with the "Gulf Stream," a date with God.

Consider the experience of a man who, like Abraham, went out, not knowing whither he went.

St. Paul had seen a vision of a man needing help, as many men have seen it. He sailed from Troas to Philippi. On arriving he had to face the disappointment of what must have seemed an anticlimax. He found no multitude waiting at the port. There were just a few

28

women holding a prayer meeting. A pretty slim beginning for the evangelization of a continent! But, also, God was at the dock to meet him.

As it was in the beginning—so now. You have a date with a God who will meet you on any landing beach. If men can go into action of any sort with that assurance as the deepest thing in their minds and hearts, they go in force.

11 ✿ Life Begins at Forty

W HEN ONE reads these words about Moses' walking into his lifework when he was forty years of age (Acts 7:23), the mind bounces off like a billiard ball to the title of a book of many seasons back, *Life Begins at Forty*. However true or false that statement may be as a universal generalization, it is true that life did begin for Moses at forty. That was not because he had reached any magic day on the calendar, but because, when he was forty, he began to get about a bit. He began to poke into things and see what was happening in his world. He got out from behind the barricade of a king's palace and down into the brickyard where his brothers were driven under the lash. He escaped from the royal routine of "peace, perfect peace," and got into the midst of a labor struggle.

Life began for Moses when he got on the rim of his world, when he began to grow in awareness of people and of what life meant to them. That is when life in the fullest sense begins for anyone. This is not a matter of duty, charity, kindness, so much as of intellectual adventurousness. It is the dedication of the imagination to social ends. It is the projection of mind into the lives of others, so that we get a real feel of the burdens which cut cruelly into other shoulders.

Life began for Moses when he got into a fight. That is when life begins for anyone. To say this is not to stress the virtues of pugnacity; it has none. Nor is it to extol the oversimplification of the complex issues of life and society into clear, sharp black-and-white; that is a delusion which easily besets radicals and reformers. It is rather the feeling of moral alternatives, the response to the struggle of humanity which pulls on something deeper than reason.

Life began for Moses when he stopped strolling as a neutral observer and became part of a struggle for justice and human right. It is the reddest of red-letter days in the life of anyone when he gets down from the grandstand into the arena of life.

12 ✿ "Shrink or Expand"

LORD CHESTERFIELD deserves our gratitude for saying, in his *Letters to My Son*, so many things that are simply not true. Thus we can see them and reject his advice. Someone has well said that he brought to the business of giving advice to young men the manners of a dancing master and the morals of a prostitute.

One thing Chesterfield advised his son to do was this: *"Always shrink yourself to the size of the company you are in."* That ought to take a Pulitzer prize for poor advice. Of course, there is this much sense to it, the wisdom of talking to people on some common ground which they share with you. Thus, if a man is an expert in higher mathematics, he ought to leave that subject out in conversation with a regular member of the human race, and talk to people on the basis of their common interests.

But Lord Chesterfield did not mean anything as sensible as that. He meant what he said: When you are in the company of people, always shrink yourself to their size, no matter how small it is. Thus many men do strike the lowest common denominator of the crowd they are in, and shrink themselves in a tragic way, leaving out the best that they are and can be.

It is a bad thing to shrink yourself so that you leave out the memory of the best people you have ever known, people whose lives and personality have been forces that have kept you up to your best. Keep them alive in you; carry them with you into any company. Don't shrink yourself; *expand* yourself to your true possible moral stature. Don't leave your best self at home.

13 ✿ *What Is It All About?*

JAMES TRUSLOW ADAMS, the American historian, wrote this: "Perhaps it would be a good idea, fantastic as it sounds, to muffle every telephone, halt every motor, and stop all activity some day, to give people a chance to ponder for a few minutes on what it is all about, why they are living and what they really want."

It would be hard to think of one sentence which would put more strongly the case for worship and church attendance. That is what worship does, among other things—it gives us a chance to think what life is all about.

Keeping Six Clocks Ticking Together

WHEN CHARLES V, the Holy Roman Emperor in the sixteenth century, retired, he spent six years in his palace in Spain, trying to make six clocks tick together. He could not do it. Then remembering the problems of Europe, he said: "How can I make six nations tick together?"

It is a memorable picture of the poor old king, evidently with his mind impaired, putting in the days and years at the momentous task of trying to make clocks tick together!

It seems an impossible task, and in his day it was. But electricity has brought a new day. It is no longer impossible. The Western Union Telegraph Company does it every day, and makes not only six clocks ticks together, but makes many times sixty thousand clocks tick together. It does the trick by calling in the sky, the sun, and the stars. The clocks all tick together because they are regulated by astronomy. The time comes from the Naval Observatory in Washington, and the clocks have the same time because they all get their time from the heavens.

That is the only dependable way to make true harmony. It is true in a family. The members may be at cross purposes unless they all respond to some common purpose, the welfare of the family, rather than to the selfish purpose of individual advantage. When Christ is truly the head of the home, the members "tick" together.

The same is true of a church. In the first Christian century in the church at Corinth, the Apostle Paul found ferocious disharmony, the whole fellowship rent by party cries. In his wonderful thirteenth chapter of First Corinthians he showed them that the way to get along together was for each to be regulated by the love of Christ. That is the only cure for antagonism and rivalry in a church, or between churches or denominations.

The same is true of nations in the world. Each tends to tick at its own time. Only by finding a common compulsion to action, in something larger than their own advantage—that is, in the righteousness and justice of God—will they ever "tick together."

15 ❊ "Thou Shouldst be Living at This Hour"

T HE WORDS above, of course, are from Wordsworth's great sonnet on Milton.

> Milton, thou shouldst be living at this hour.
> England hath need of thee . . .

It is one of the great poems of the English language. It raises a penetrating question: What sort of people would be called back to earth in a time of great need of humanity? If we answer that question, we get a sure line on the people who really count.

Think of the men who set out to conquer the world. There is Alexander the Great. Can you think of anyone crying: "Alexander, thou shouldst be living at this hour?" Would anyone say: "Napoleon, thou shouldst be living at this hour?" Who but a blind and dumb man would call back Napoleon, about whom Victor Hugo gave the massive verdict: "God got tired of him"?

Or take riches. There is John Jacob Astor, the first multimillionaire in America. Can we hear anyone saying: Astor, thou shouldst be living at this hour"? The truth is, men feel that things are bad enough in the world without cluttering it up with any of the great despoilers and brigands of the past, no matter how famous.

But how many people we would call back, if possible! Again and again men feel and say of Lincoln, of Luther, of Jane Addams, of Phillips Brooks and an unnumbered host unknown to fame: "Thou shouldst be living at this hour!"

Can we think of anyone asking, after we have gone, "Return to us"? What makes a person worthy of a return performance? The poem itself gives a satisfactory answer:

Thy soul was like a star, and dwelt apart . . .
So didst thou travel in life's common way,
In cheerful godliness; and yet thy heart
The lowliest duties on herself did lay.

   There it is—two things. One is "cheerful godliness," the sense of
relationship to God carried into life. The other is the acceptance of
duties. Anyone whose life shows these qualities wins the accolade:
"Come back."

16 ❖ Molehills Out of Mountains

SOMETIMES WE get a new view of truth by standing an idea on its head, or putting it into reverse. That is certainly true of the common phrase, "making mountains out of molehills." It is a good description of people we all know; fussy, timorous, magnifying trifles until they look like the Alps.

But there is a worse thing than that. It is to make molehills out of mountains. Many do that. They treat great truths of moral majesty as though they were little hillocks of no importance at all. Such people get their magnitudes mixed. They make small things great and great things small. They spend their lives acquiring the means of living, and disregard the ends which might give some meaning to the means.

Consider the greatest thing in life, *the knowledge of God*, "whom to know aright is life eternal."

That is the Mount Everest of human life. Yet it is possible to make a molehill out of it, a little thing to which one gives no real attention year in and year out.

Consider how the philosopher William James rated that knowledge of God as a great mountain in his words: "We and God have business with each other; and in opening ourselves to His influence, our deepest destiny is fulfilled." What a blunder to make a molehill out of that!

Those who disregard *the moral disciplines of life* make a molehill out of a great mountain! They think of discipline and self-control as old-fashioned, narrow, or Puritanical. They go in for quantity, not quality of life. When there are no high moral or ethical mountains in their life's landscape, their motto becomes: "Eat, drink, and be merry." They can manage the first two, but not the last.

Often a molehill is made out of a real mountain—*service to humanity*. That, with many people, comes in as incidental, if at all. It never looms as a commanding height, whose climbing is life's great achievement. Their lives sound out three little words: I, me, and mine. Very little words! Think of the people who have forgotten themselves into immortality through service; not only the roll of the famous, but the anonymous great known fully only to God.

Have we gotten our magnitudes all mixed up? Here is a true measurement: let the things which were great to Jesus be great to us, and the thing which were small to him be small to us.

17 ❖ Danger Ahead—Marriage!

IN THE first edition of her novel, *The Age of Innocence*, Edith
Wharton made a glaring mistake in quoting as part of the Marriage Service in the Prayer Book, what was really the opening
part of the ritual for the Burial Service.

There is much in that mistake worth thinking about. For it may
picture a common sort of tragedy. That is, marriage may become
a sort of burial, in which the parties may be laid away, as far as any
deep interest in life, other than that of their own home, is concerned.
If the true facts in regard to some marriages were incorporated in
a marriage service, the ritual might possibly be something like this:
"Forasmuch as John and Mary have consented in Holy Matrimony,
we consign their bodies to a tomb of a five-room house, without
windows on the world."

For what starts out as a "honeymoon cottage" may become a prison
for the spirit. There may be so exclusive a type of happiness that
the four walls become prison walls, and the music may be the *true*
"Prisoner's Song": "Let the rest of the world go by." The couple
may retire from any kind of costly service to other people, wrapped
up in their own self-concern.

Another danger of marriage is that it may be conducive to making
almost the whole of life consist in *things*. There are so many things
a home needs: electric refrigerator, vacuum cleaner, hot water
heater, and later, a crib and a world of accessories, that the mood—
"I can't bother about anyone else. I'm loaded with expenses. We
can't subscribe a cent till we get the last payment made"—may become a permanent one. Their world becomes a world of "thing-full
emptiness." Then we may ask, "What shall it profit a man and a
woman, if they gain the whole world of gadgets, and lose their own
lives."

A third danger ahead in marriage is that the children in the home, instead of increasing the interest of the parents in *all* children, will lead them to act as if their children were *the only children in the world*.

18 ✿ Image Making and Breaking

ONE OF the most powerful forces that act on every one of us is the image of ourselves that we carry around with us inside of our heads in our imagination. That's why we call it imagination—that's the part of our mind that furnishes images for us to look at.

The chief handicap that many people have is not a poor brain, but the wrong pictures of themselves, which come to dominate them. For instance, many a man is paralyzed in his actions because he has a negative image. He has told himself so often, "I can't do it," that he gets an image of himself as a person who can't do things and the image prevents him from putting forth a real effort.

A wise man said, "We tend to become what we imagine ourselves to be." That is true. A track coach once made a pole vault man put in his room a picture of himself clearing the bar in fine form, not because he wanted the man to become conceited, but because he knew that the deciding factor in the man's performance would be the idea in the man's mind of what he could do. He wanted to make that positive image of the man doing a successful job dominant in his mind. And it worked!

One of the biggest things Jesus did for men was to break up negative images they had of themselves and substitute positive images. He was both an image-breaker and an image-maker. For instance, there was Peter, "Thou art Cephas," Jesus said. "Thou shalt be Peter." Jesus broke up the image that Zacchaeus had of himself as an outcast, a corrupt politician, and made a new image in which he saw himself as a son of God. Zacchaeus lived up to the new rating put upon himself.

Jesus still performs the crucial service for people. Many a man has a sort of image of himself as an animal. That is, the physical sensations of all sorts are the things which bulk largest in his scheme

41

of life. But if Jesus really comes into a man's mind, he breaks that image. He says convincingly, "You are a son of God. You are more than a collection of animal sensations. You can live up to the level of the new image of yourself, which is the true one." Or another man has allowed the chief image of himself in his own thinking to be that of a failure. "There's no use," he says to himself, "I'm no good." As long as that image controls, he will be no good. But when that man accepts the message of Jesus, a new picture is formed, that of a man who by the grace of God can bring power and moral distinction into his life.

19 ❈ *Tolerance or Rubber Spine?*

OGDEN NASH, in a quatrain, expresses wonder whether the tolerance on which he prides himself is really tolerance or just the effect of having a rubber spine.

That is a good question to ask ourselves in an age when tolerance has been regarded by many people as the supreme virtue. Many people flatter themselves that they have the shining virtue of tolerance when what they really have is lack of courage and conviction. Of course, intolerance, in the sense of bigoted denunciation of every view and idea except our own, is a terrible evil. It has wrought immeasurable harm in the world; it has caused cruel persecution, the Inquisition, the execution of people for their opinions. In our own time we have seen its colossal evils in the totalitarian states, in Nazi Germany, Fascist Italy, and Communist Russia.

Today, however, the word often stands for an easygoing indifference of a person who really does not care about the moral quality of things. That is not "tolerance"; it is merely selfish unconcern.

In the presence of great evils we need more than a rubber spine, which buckles under when we are attacked or disputed. We need what might truly be called the "intolerance" of Jesus. He vigorously opposed those who "devoured widows' houses." He could not "tolerate" them because he loved people and hated the greed that oppressed them. He could not tolerate those who injured "little ones" and caused them to do evil. In like manner, Wilberforce was intolerant of human slavery. There are glaring evils among us today to which we should never get comfortably adjusted. That means we are unconcerned about the evil that is done to others as long as our own skins are safe.

Just run your hand up and down your back. Do you have a stiff, rugged backbone or a "rubber spine"?

20 ❖ *Handshakes Across the Years*

RICHARD L. ALDINGTON, the British poet who has been living in the United States for several years, has, in his autobiography, a speculation about handshakes which contains much food for thought. He writes, playfully, that he is sure he is a real poet, because he is only five handshakes away from Shelley.

He goes on to prove it: he once shook hands with the poet Swinburne, who once shook hands with the poet Southey, who in turn shook hands with Walter Savage Landor, who was an intimate friend of Shelley. So he figured he was only five handshakes away from Shelley.

That is a game we can all play. Anyone who has ever shaken hands with an ordained Methodist preacher can truly say that he is only six handshakes away from John Wesley. The preacher shook hands with some bishop, and that bishop shook hands with an older bishop of a preceding generation.

That will bring us to three handshakes from Bishop Matthew Simpson, who shook hands with Bishop William McKendree. McKendree was ordained by Francis Asbury, who in turn was sent out to America by John Wesley. We can be sure that Wesley shook hands with Asbury when he said good-by. That brings us to six handshakes from Wesley.

So, in the same way, we can figure that we are all within five or six handshakes from Thomas Jefferson, and not more than eleven or twelve from Martin Luther.

What a short distance, measured by handshakes!

The big question that arises, however, is how far is the distance measured by *spirit*? Take Jefferson, for instance. Only five handshakes away. But how far away are we in spirit and practice from the man who believed desperately in democracy?

Only five handclasps from Wesley. How far are we from his spirit, who said: "Fear nothing but sin"? How far are we in spirit from Luther, and his magnificent courage and devotion? Close the gap!

21 ❖ The Age of Collecting

A LARGE ADVERTISEMENT in a daily newspaper not long ago was headed by these words in large print: MAGIC NUMBERS 20 TO 40.

There was a bit of mystery about it, so the reader went on to find out what the advertiser meant by "magic numbers." Of course he wanted to sell something, lots of things. The magic numbers, 20 to 40, represented the "age of collecting and accumulation." During these years people accumulate things, young couples start a home, bring up children, buy the household gear that will furnish a home. It sounds reasonable. The only doubt about it is that the limit of "collecting" was set at forty. People go on accumulating all their lives. A woman in New England had been collecting antiques until, in her nineties, she became one herself.

But there are worthier things than the contents of a large department store. For if all our collecting is merely of objects, we may end up with the verdict Jesus gave on a prominent "collector" in that time: the Rich Fool. Jesus called him a fool. He was. He spent his whole time in collecting barns filled with food.

Here are some items to accumulate, if life is to be a true success:

Collect some questions. It is more important to ask the right questions than it is to know all the answers. Jenner, for instance, when England was ravaged by smallpox, noticed that the one group of people who did not get smallpox was milkmaids. He asked why, and kept on asking till he got the answer. Thus smallpox was ultimately wiped out, because Jenner learned to inoculate against it. So we must accumulate persistent questions, such as: "Must the world go on with the old pattern of slaughter? What is the meaning of life?"

Collect some worries. No doubt the fine old Quaker word "concern" is a better word than worry. Too many people never get concerned over anything but their own welfare and prestige. There is too much routine living and too little real concern over the world. Jesus knew the peace of God. He also was deeply disturbed over need and suffering.

Collect some debts. Every one of us could say to that: "Don't worry. I have plenty." So we have. Yet men often lack any real sense of being in debt to others who have labored and into whose labors they have entered. Longfellow writes of the Village Blacksmith:

> He looks the whole world in the face
> For he owes not any man.

The answer to that is "Nonsense!" He is deeply in debt to the pioneers who through the centuries discovered iron and the way to use it. The privilege of owning a blacksmith shop in security he owed to all the hosts who had fought for and created the common law of England, and the guards of freedom. Give to your life the exhilaration that comes from a sense of obligation to all from whose hands we have received the unearned gifts that have blessed our lives. Through St. Paul's life there ran a great melody—"I am debtor." That feeling of debt will give humility and save from the corroding evils of pride and conceit.

Accumulate a faith to live by. Far too many people have something to live *on* but little or nothing to live *by*.

22 ❈ Zigzagging Through Life

ADMIRAL BYRD, on his second trip to the region of the South Pole, flew down along the 180th meridian of longitude in the Pacific. That is the international date line, an imaginary boundary. When a ship crosses it, a day is either added or subtracted. On one side of the line, for instance, it is Wednesday, and on the other side it is Thursday.

In writing about it, Admiral Richard E. Byrd uses a striking phrase: "All the time we were continually flying as closely as possible along the 180th meridian. Even without wind-drift, for which adequate correction could be made, it is obvious that no navigator could fly along a mathematical line. Consequently, since this is the international date line, we were zigzagging constantly from today into tomorrow and back again."

A striking idea—"zigzagging into tomorrow and back again." When we pay a life insurance premium, or buy a house, or have a medical examination, we dip into the future, thinking of the needs of tomorrow as well as of today. We go into the future in our planning, and then back into the midst of today.

But the phrase has high meaning in a larger sense, that life can be, and should be, a zigzag into eternity and back into time. We may turn our minds to the things that are eternal, to the God who has been the dwelling place of men in all generations, and then, with quickened vision and restored soul, we can come back to the immediate tasks of the present moment and day.

That, of course, is what happens in real worship. We withdraw into eternity and come back into time.

We zigzag into eternity through meditation and the study of God's revelation in the Bible. A Hebrew rabbi used to dismiss his classes with the explanation: "Such are my engagements with myself that I shall be too busy for other things." We need that kind of "engagements" with ourselves that give opportunity for the things that are eternal to become real and powerful in our lives.

Jesus himself is the best example of zigzagging through life. "He went up into a mountain to pray." Then he came down again for service amid the pressing crowd. His life was replenished in God, and out of that fullness he gave without measure.

Aldous Huxley has said a memorable word on this whole matter: "It is only by deliberately paying our attention and our primary allegiance to eternity that we can prevent time from turning our lives into a pointless and diabolical foolery."

23 ❉ "Dead Money"

IN BANKING circles the phrase above, "dead money," has a specific, technical meaning. It is used to describe the forgotten money on deposit in national banks. We might think, offhand, that people who put money in the bank would certainly remember it. But that is by no means true. National banks alone hold fifty million dollars in 2,329,678 accounts whose owners are never heard from. There it is, fifty million dollars on the books or in the vaults— dead!

But that amount, certainly, is not the only kind of dead money. Excavations in the Mediterranean area have turned up another tragic kind of money that has been "dead" for centuries. The author of the fascinating book, *Gods, Graves and Scholars*, has written of the excavation of the city of Pompeii, which was buried in the lava from Mt. Vesuvius. "The first body uncovered stretched out full length was a skeleton, with gold and silver coins that had rolled out of bony hands, still seeking, it seemed, to clutch them fast." A tragic picture; a person, even in the last gasp of death, clutching to gold!

Beyond that, in the Christian view of life, there is another sort of dead money—that which is never invested in human life. The Biblical phrase: "Passed from death unto life," may apply to a person's pocketbook as well as to a person's soul. How much of our money is "dead" in that sense, so that it never ministers to the lives of people?

When we raise this question we need to keep our wits about us and not get bogged down into sentimentalism. Not all the money we spend on ourselves is dead money, by any means. In a very real way, our first duty is to ourselves. It is our responsibility to contribute to the world the best-equipped person we can, in health, strength, and ability. Whatever goes into such an equipment is money in the service to human life.

That is a very different thing from putting money into ostentation, or grasping acquisition, or holding a dollar so close to our eyes that we can see nothing else. Cleveland Amory in a recent article in *Holiday* quotes a Mr. Moneybags as saying to his wife at Bar Harbor, Maine, in a sharp complaint: "My dear, you are not spending enough money." That was a natural feeling, we suppose, in a summer resort where competition in display was the order of the day, and where one woman outdistanced all others by putting in solid gold bathtub fixtures! That was dead money.

One woman once complained that she did not like to go down to the safe deposit vault of her bank because it looked like a mausoleum. That is what it may be, a graveyard for dead money laid away in tombs!

In regard to our possessions, we need the old miracle of the Garden of Eden. "God breathed into man's nostrils the breath of life, and he became a living soul." If we allow God to breathe the breath of life into our pocketbook, it, too, can become a living and life-giving power.

24 ❊ "How Do You Play It?"

THE *New Yorker* magazine once published a striking cartoon, with the characteristic type of humor which it has popularized, which arouses mirth by the force of sheer absurdity. At the game counter of a department store, a solid, serious matron has bought something, and the clerk is making out the sales slip. The woman's eye has idly caught sight of a chessboard spread out on the counter with the chessmen all arranged on it. She casually asks the clerk: "How do you play it?"

Imagine asking a clerk in a store to tell her in a minute how to play chess. Some people have put in a lifetime learning how to play it well. Chess is not tiddlywinks. No one ever learns to play chess even passably without hours and days and months of real study and effort. Chess is more like algebra than it is like dominoes. Its mastery demands the expenditure of blood, sweat and tears. Well, at least sweat and tears. It can't be learned in a minute.

From here the mind trails off to parallels, and there are many, to that casual inquiry, "How do you play it?" Some things—and they are the most important things in life—can be learned only by dedicated effort.

There is prayer, for instance. Prayer as a power, a sustaining and creating force, is not learned on the spot. It takes the practice and habit of years. It is always pitiful to see people, confronted with disaster or tragedy, turning to prayer as though they could learn its power in a few moments, when they had paid no real attention to it for years. A woman, looking over the devastation which the New England hurricane of 1938 had wrought on a college campus, bringing down trees that had stood for a hundred years, said, whimsically and sadly: "You cannot improvise a tree." Nor can you improvise a habit of prayer.

The same is true of the use of the Bible. It does not become a light unto our feet and a lamp unto our path in a moment. To the question: "How do you play it?" the only valid answer is: "You must live with it. It is a great instrument, but like the violin, it must be learned with toil."

So it is with a Christian home. People often look enviously at the children in a Christian home, children in whom Christian truth and character have been carried over from one generation to the next, and ask the parents: "How do you do it?" Outsiders seem to feel that such a tremendous result is caused by some kind of a little magic twist, something that can be done in a few weeks. It can only be done with the expenditure of love, of restraint, of discipline and of prayer.

25 ❖ "No Faith in the Future"

WHILE a company of people were having dinner together, one man in the party, who had spent many summers in Maine, fascinated his companions by telling of his experiences with a little town named Flagstaff, in the months before it was to be flooded, as part of a large lake for which a dam was being built. All improvements and repairs in the whole town were stopped. What was the use of painting a house if it were to be covered with water in six months? Why repair anything when the whole village was to be wiped out? So, week by week, the whole town became more and more bedraggled, more gone to seed, more woebegone. Then he added by way of explanation: "Where there is no faith in the future, there is no power in the present."

That word is a profound one, and has a far wider application than merely to the flooding of a town. Of course, it applied with crystal clearness to that little town of Flagstaff. The people of Flagstaff had no faith in the future and, of course, had no power in the present.

It applies to our world right now. So many people are very close to despair over the possibility of a third world war and of wiping the human race off the planet. There are some couples who are even refusing to have children, because they fear they would just be blown to bits. A dire consequence of this is a lack of power in the present. This is a completely unchristian state of mind and heart. It practically says that God is dead, or will not be a factor in the world from now on. We should not minimize the seriousness of the hour, or pretend that it is not dangerous. But if we are Christians we must not leave God out of our world. For the final question is not what Russia is going to do, but what *God* is going to do. Our world has not slipped out of God's pocket. It is still in His shaping hands. We need that deep faith if we are to confront our world today with anything other than despair. Otherwise we have no power in the present with which to arm ourselves for action to make God's will prevail.

The same is true of our attitude to the Church. There are some within the Church, perhaps a large number, who do not have a stout faith in its future. They think and act as though it were a losing venture. They look at the obstacles, and there are many and staggering ones: the collapse of China, the disregard of religion in such large parts of Europe, the frequent lack of drive and devotion among church people in the United States, the slow movement toward church unity. That distrust is one reason for the lack of power in the present. We need a faith that God never gets down to His last nickel, that His Church is the Body of Christ and will not be left without His power and direction. Faith in God's tomorrow will bring strength to our action in God's today. Vachel Lindsay has put the questions, and the answer, in noble poetry:

> What is the final ending?
> The issue, who can know?
> Will Christ outlive Mohammed?
> Will Kali's altars go?
>
> This is our faith tremendous,—
> Our wild hope, who shall scorn—
> That in the name of Jesus
> The world shall be reborn! [1]

[1] "Foreign Missions in Battle Array," from *The Collected Poems of Vachel Lindsay*. Used by permission of The Macmillan Company.

26 ✿ *Outliving Yourself*

THERE ARE two striking lines in one of the stanzas of that great hymn, sung frequently during the Lenter season, "O Sacred Head, now wounded." They are:

> Lord, may I never, never,
> Outlive my love to Thee.

Think them over.

There are so many things which it is a tragedy, in some ways, to outlive. It is always sad for a person to outlive his generation, to be "the last leaf upon the tree." Oliver Wendell Holmes gives a poignant picture:

> And if I should live to be
> The last leaf upon the tree
> In the spring,
> Let them smile, as I do now,
> At the old forsaken bough,
> Where I cling.

It is tragic, in a real sense, to outlive one's strength, to outlive one's money, and to learn how steep are unfamiliar stairs. It is a hard experience to outlive all of one's family.

But there is something more tragic than that. It is to outlive one's *self*. A poet once wrote truly: "I have outlived myself by many a year." Lord Byron, once required to write his age in a registry book, wrote: "Age, 100." That was the way he felt. He, too, had outlived himself. To outlive the best one has known and done, to outlive one's highest aspiration, his deepest dedication, his richest joy—that is true tragedy. Also, an unmatched calamity, as the hymn puts it, is to outlive our love of God.

27 ❋ *False Promises*

THERE IS one sentence in the story of the temptation of Jesus which deserves more attention than it usually receives. It is the promise made by Satan to Jesus in the third temptation. After showing him the kingdoms of the world and their glory, he said, "All these will I give thee, if thou wilt fall down and worship me."

In those words, as usual, Satan lied. The kingdoms of the world were not really his to give. The kingdoms of this world belong, in the final sense, to the King of Kings and Lord of Lords, not to Satan. Of course, it was a real temptation. There are temporary elements of power and earthly grandeur which can be seized by accepting the rule of evil. The "conquerors" of earth have demonstrated that in their brief hours of glory. Jesus resisted that temptation, as he resisted the others, by bringing the word of God to bear. He replied: "Thou shalt worship the Lord thy God, and Him only shalt thou serve."

That same false promise of evil has been repeated again and again. Satan offers to all of us what is really not in his power to give. We can see that clearly in three realms.

Security is something all men desire. Evil says: "I will give you security through wealth. Get enough dollars and you will have no worries about anything else. Push yourself along, dig your elbows into others, trample on anyone who gets in your way, and you will have all you need." What a lie, as has been proved in millions of lives. We can have millions, and if we are "not rich toward God," we will be only rich fools. What security does mere wealth give against boredom, futility, sickness, the absence of true fellowship, and, finally, death?

Happiness is a goal we all strive to reach. Evil says: "I will give you happiness through pleasure. Indulge every desire, let yourself go without any restrictions, and you will be happy." How can anyone believe that lie? Happiness is not in Satan's power to give. The true happiness of life is to be found in a set of directions which begins: "Blessed are the poor in spirit."

Freedom is another thing universally desired. Satan steals up on us in our thinking and says: "I will make you free. Cast off any and all obligations. Don't wear any chains of any kind. Be your own boss." How many people have ruined their lives by listening to such deceptive promises! The broad Liberty Highway which they took, ended them in a prison cell, prisoners of their own physical instincts and whims of the hour. There is only one true way to freedom in the deepest sense. It is found in the words of Jesus: "Ye shall know the truth, and the truth shall make you free." It is found in the words proudly recorded by St. Paul: "Paul, a prisoner of Jesus Christ."

28 ❖ *How Do You Talk to Yourself?*

SOME PEOPLE may think they can answer this question by saying: "I do not talk to myself!" But of course you do. We all spend most of our time talking to ourselves. Not vocally, necessarily, although there is quite a lot of that. We all have repeated interior debates with ourselves, debates which determine action and character. So the question, "How do you talk to yourself?" has real meaning for each of us. We ought to listen to ourselves critically, to learn what kind of advice we give to ourselves. The suggestions which follow are not accusations, but observations.

Some people put in much time in *self-congratulation*. Thus they whisper to themselves: "That was a beautiful job you did! Really, you are a wonder!" It does not take many doses of that poisonous stuff to make a person swell up like a pouter pigeon.

Some people wallow in *self-pity*. They say to themselves: "You poor thing! You have had a tough time! Everything is against you. People are in a conspiracy against your success." In such a deluge of pity for oneself, the will and spirit crumble.

Other people are right there with *an excuse for every mistake they make*, for every sin they commit. They have ever-ready alibis for themselves. Their wrongdoing is not really their fault! They were compelled by outside forces over which they had no control! Consequently, they can never say those great words: "I have sinned." Shakespeare describes this tribe of excuse-makers in a marvelous passage in *King Lear*, Act I, scene II: "This is the excellent foppery of the world, that, when we are sick in fortune—often the surfeit of our own behavior—we make guilty of our disasters the sun, the moon, the stars, as if we are villains by necessity; fools by heavenly compulsion, knaves, thieves, and poachers by spherical predominance; liars, drunkards, and adulterers by an enforced obedience of planetary influence."

But there are other ways of talking to ourselves which develop character, rather than ruin it. Some people hold themselves up to their best by the way they talk to themselves. They keep the high mark of their calling in clear view. They speak, in the words of the hymn: "My soul, be on thy guard."

We can bring *reinforcement* to ourselves by the way in which we talk to ourselves. There is a marvelous picture of this in Psalms 42:

> Why are you cast down, O my soul,
>   and why are you disquieted within me?
> Hope in God; for I shall again praise him,
>   my help and my God.

That is a good line of conversation!

29 ❊ *Living Upside Down*

I N ANY list of strange animals, there will nearly always be included the giant sloth, which lives in trees and for the most part lives upside down. The encyclopedia records this fact: "Sloths sleep, eat, and travel through the forest upside down." They are not found in North America. So far as we know, the whole animal family in North America is right side up!

It is a suggestive idea—*living upside down!* The two-toed sloth and the three-toed sloth do it. There are also hosts of people who, in many important and real ways, seem to do much of their living upside down. The things that ought to be on top in their lives are pushed way down to the bottom. Their values are topsy-turvy. The beautiful verses of Harry Kemp picture the most important thing in man's nature and life. He writes that the "upward reach" is the chief of God's "wondrous works."

But often that upward reach is held down and attention given entirely to the things of the downward look, to the earth. The "upside" man, his head, is often put down below the power of physical instincts. It was said of the early apostles that they "turned the world upside down." That was because the wrong things were on top. They wished in the name and by the power of God to put the world right side up.

30 ❖ *Minority Reports*

ONCE IN a while one comes across a sentence in a newspaper which shines like a quotation from the New Testament in illuminated letters. One such sentence was that in *The New York Times* recently in a review of a volume of letters of Beatrice Webb. Speaking of Mrs. Webb and her husband, Sidney Webb, Lord Passmore, the students of labor, and political leaders in Great Britain, the reviewer wrote: "They signed many minority reports which became majority actions."

What higher praise could a person ever win than to stand for a good cause with a minority until it grew to be a majority! The sentence stimulates the imagination, for there is so much history in it. That is part of the business of the Church—to bring in minority reports against evil, reports which later become majority actions. The Christian Church began that way. It brought in a minority report against the custom in the Greek and Roman world of exposing unwanted babies to the weather, in other words, murdering them. The Christian teaching awakened the conscience of the people and the minority position did become the majority action.

It was the same with the protest of the Christians against the barbarous gladiatorial fights. The Christians were a pitifully small minority. What did a tiny group of protestors count, against the roars of 100,000 spectators enjoying the brutal murders in the Coloseum? Well, they counted enough to stop the gladiators in a few score years. So with other minority reports, such as those against human slavery and against the cruel oppression of child laborers.

Our business today is to bring in minority reports against great evils and to fight on in the faith that under the power of God such reports will become majority actions. Napoleon had a good word to say, which applies here, on the power of a few people of determination. Speaking of the American Revolution, he said: "The greatest issues of the world were decided by the skirmishes of picket guards."

True! Join the picket guards!

31 ✿ *"J'm All Alone"*

TIME MAGAZINE recorded a remark made by Mrs. Cornelius Vanderbilt, Sr., which is worth a second look, a third look, and a tenth look. *Time* gave the following background:

> After her husband's death in 1942, Grace Vanderbilt abandoned to the wreckers the 58-room Fifth Avenue mansion which had cost her husband's grandfather $1,000,000 to build in 1881. Resettled farther up Fifth Avenue in a 28-room pile, which she termed "The Gardener's Cottage," Mrs. Vanderbilt lost none of her queenly manner. Convinced that the Vanderbilts were a breed apart, she sometimes described herself as "all alone in the house," when there were, in fact, 18 servants with her.

Think that over! "All alone"—except for the little item of eighteen other people. They were servants, of course; but they were also members of the family of God. This, surely, is one of the most terrible afflictions that can happen to a person: to be so wrapped up in himself that he thinks of himself as "all alone" even when surrounded by people, his brothers and sisters. It is on the spiritual and intellectual level of the tribe of Eskimos found by Donald MacMillan, the arctic explorer, who thought of themselves as the only people in the world!

We are not alone. We are bound up in one bundle of life, as the truth is so beautifully expressed in I Samuel 25. If and when we deny being part of this one bundle of life, a terrible punishment is inflicted upon us. We are condemned to solitary confinement. Bernard Shaw has written: "The worst sin against our fellow creatures is not to hate them, but to be indifferent to them: that's the essence of inhumanity."

Jesus, in his opening sermon at Nazareth, announced that he had come to bring "release to the captives." He does bring release from that terrible kind of captivity—the captivity to self.

We are not alone. There are lives all around us, and other lives far away, to whom we are bound as brothers and sisters in Christ. Like St. Paul, we are debtors to them all, to the Greeks and to the barbarians. We owe them love. This may well lead into a thought of the "God of the Lonely" which may include those who make themselves lonely by their own choice.

32 ✿ *A Human Chain*

ONE SPECIALTY of the melodramas, produced back in the days when the prices in many theaters were ten, twenty, and thirty cents, was the rescue of the beautiful heroine by a chain of men. One man would stand on the shoulders of another and a second man on his shoulders. Then they would fall across a chasm to make a human bridge over which the heroine escaped to safety from the clutches of the villain amid loud cheers from the audience.

Sometimes this, or something like it, happens in real life. One such rescue was reported in a news story from Wales. The story was still melodrama, but it was true. Here is a bit of it, from the Associated Press:

ABERCRAVE, WALES—A chain of 85 men pulled two explorers to safety tonight from a flooded underground Welsh cave where they had been trapped for three days.

The two men had been imprisoned deep inside a cavern under mountains. A sudden rainstorm sent down tons of water and blocked all exits from the cave. Deep sea divers plunged through the stream to reach the explorers. Then a human chain was formed through the swift underground water.

Such a story is more than a curiosity in the news. It pictures, without any stretching, one of the basic facts of human life and society; behind every life there is a human chain of other lives. We have all been rescued by a chain of more than eighty-five people. "Others have labored and we have entered into their labors." This applies not only to immediate ancestors but to a host of people, many of them unknown and unseen, whose lives have influenced ours.

That truth should bring to us a sense both of humility and obligation. We ought to be humble, because we do not stand "on our own" but we all have a chain of people behind us. How silly and insufferable it would have been for these two explorers, after the rescue, to boast: "That was a fine job *we* did!" Is it any more silly than the boast of many thoughtless folks who proclaim that they are "self-made men"? That is the emptiest chatter that anyone can utter. We have little that we have not received. May we acknowledge with gratitude and humility the gifts of God which have come through the human chain behind and around us.

Also such a remembrance should bring a sense of obligation. "Freely you have received, freely give." We can all be part of a chain which makes possible fine achievements in other lives. Every noble thing ever done has been the result of the cooperation of many people. Take the conversion of St. Paul, for instance. What a network of lives there was for that, each one contributing a vital part! There were the men who led him, when blinded by the vision on the road, into Damascus. There was Judas, who opened his home to Paul; there was the noble Ananias, who stretched forth his hand, in spite of all the cruel persecution which Paul had led, and called him "Brother Saul." How different the story of Paul might have been without these people, many of them obscure, who formed a human chain to help the vision become the continuing reality of his life. Think of the far-reaching results of the word of the Sunday-school teacher who first brought to Dwight L. Moody the idea of giving his life to Christian service. It is a sobering question. Are we a part of any human chain over which others may pass from an old life to a new one?

33 ❋ "Let the Rest of the World Go By"

THE SAME words often have utterly different meanings. A man had the following experience during a church service on Good Friday. The congregation was singing the hymn, "Beneath the Cross of Jesus, I Fain Would Take My Stand." He was struck by the words in the third stanza: "Content to let the world go by." His mind flashed back to recall a similar line in a popular song of years ago: "Let the rest of the world go by." The same words—but how different! In the popular song the words, although written as a love song, are the perfect expression of complete selfishness. The idea is: "Just you and I will get away somewhere, wrap ourselves up in our own affairs, and 'let the rest of the world go by'! What do we care about the troubles of the world or the suffering and need of people? This is nothing to us as long as we are safe in our little hide-out."

How different in attitude are the words: "Content to let the world go by." We will not be disturbed by joining in the frantic and feverish chase of the things of the world—money, comfort, or fame. All these we will be content to let go by because of the higher prize of the "excellency of Christ Jesus" and of being a part of God's love and aid to the needy of the world. We may well ask ourselves: Just how do we "let the rest of the world go by"? May we be able truly to sing with all our hearts and minds:

> Content to let the world go by
> To know no gain or loss;
> My sinful self my only shame,
> My glory all the cross.

34 ❋ "No Business that Required Entry"

JOHN WOOLMAN'S *Journal* is one of the classics of the devotional life, a book about which Charles Lamb said: "Get the *Journal* of John Woolman by heart." In part of the *Journal* there is a mournful item that is repeated over and over. On a trip during which he visited the Friends' Societies in North Carolina, he felt a deep distress over the frequent occurrence in the minutes of the Societies' meetings of the words: "No business that required entry." Sometimes he felt heartbroken. Sometimes he grew angry, feeling: "In God's name, why was there not some business that required entry and strong action? With the sin of slavery and its cruelties all around them, and the sin of war impending, how could they say, 'No business that required entry'?"

It is a disturbing phrase. We will not find those exact words on the records of the official boards of churches. There is always business of some kind. But there is danger of coming pretty close to those words as far as the big business of the Kingdom of God is concerned. There is real danger of churches which "sit and sing themselves away," if not to everlasting bliss, at least to everlasting futility. Every church ought to have business that requires immediate entry and strong action. Particularly in these days when every denomination is afflicted with packs of watchdogs among the laymen, alert to see that nothing is done to make a more Christian industrial order or a more Christian world. There is business that demands entry in connection with racial segregation, and business regarding the threat of war and policies that are leading to war. The Church has urgent business to counteract the influence of those men, including several Senator Know-Nothings, who would "cry havoc, and let slip the dogs of war."

Just what business of the Kingdom is entered for action in your church, beyond keeping a routine going? Jesus did not say to his disciples when he left them: "Meet regularly every seven days." He said: "Go ye into all the world."

35 ❊ "I Find No Fault"

IT IS interesting to discover that in the Coptic Church (an ancient branch of the Christian Church in Egypt and parts of the Near East) Pontius Pilate is regarded as a saint. The slim basis for that high honor is that he said of Jesus: "I find no fault in this man."

That sounds very well. But it is hardly a basis for sainthood, or, for that matter, for Pilate's being accorded a rating of common decency because he did not back up his words. After saying, "I find no fault in this man," he delivered Jesus to the soldiers for crucifixion. Such words are very easy to say, but they are worthless if not backed up with acts.

There are many people today who can say truly: "I find no fault in this man," when referring to Jesus. As a matter of fact, any verbal criticism of Jesus is a very rare thing to find. However, it is very common to find people whose actions say: "I find no fault in this man, but I haven't been to his church in years." The actions will say, "I find no fault in this man, but I wouldn't lift a finger, and don't, to aid the things he cared for most."

Here is the way another man said the words, "I find no fault in this man." The same words that Pilate used, but what a difference! They are the words of Polycarp, a tribute to Jesus given just before his martyrdom. The words were a prelude to his giving up his life. Here is the record. The proconsul urged him and said, "Swear and I will release thee; curse the Christ." And Polycarp said, "Eighty and six years have I served him, and he hath done me no wrong. How then can I blaspheme my King who loved me?"

We can say with truth, "I find no fault in this man." But do we say it as Pilate said it or as Polycarp said it?

71

36 ✿ "She Knew It"

MANY WILL remember Jan Struther, the British novelist, particularly for her beautiful story during the Second World War, *Mrs. Miniver*, and for the film which was made from the novel. Jan Struther died a few years ago. Since then, attention has been given to a little poem which she had written, and which was read at her funeral. It not only reveals a rare spirit, but also has a bright light to throw on all of life. Here is the verse:

> One day my life will end; and lest
> Some whim should prompt you to review it,
> Let her who knew the subject best
> Tell you the shortest way to do it:
> Then say: "Here lies one doubly blest."
> Say: "She was happy." Say: "She knew it."

That is the sharp point—"*she knew it*." So many people who have so many of the materials of happiness do not *know* it! Instead of really knowing their happiness and being grateful for it, their eyes are roving over the fence to the seemingly greener grass far away. The spirit of thankfulness will help one to know his happiness and save life from being one long-drawn-out sigh.

It is a great truth for every Christian to know. We have all the gifts of the gospel, all the endowments which God has given to us in Christ. We ought to be happy and *know* that we are happy. We can be happy if we keep our minds alert to the wonders of God's grace. All too often we are like the American who was lost in London. He asked a policeman: "Where is Trafalgar Square?" The policeman replied: "You are in it!" So, we are in the grace of God, and ought to know it, and knowing it, be happy.

37 ✻ Landscape and "Inscape"

THE WORD "landscape" we know. The other word "inscape" has not yet achieved the dignity of getting into the dictionary. However, it is a logical word, used, and perhaps invented, by Christopher Morley. The landscape is what we see when we look outward. The "inscape" is what we see when we look within our minds and hearts. We all know, or we ought to, that, for the happiness and welfare of life, the inward view, the "inscape," is far more important than the outward landscape. Thus, when the outward view is dark and cheerless, the inward view may be radiant.

A stirring illustration of this is found in the words of Samuel Rutherford, a Scottish minister who was imprisoned for his religious stand and witness: "Jesus Christ came into my cell last night and every stone gleamed like a ruby." Do not call that poetic nonsense! In the experience of the man it was the actual fact. Stone walls did not a prison make for him. His faith brought light to a dark dungeon.

When the writer, Leigh Hunt, was sent to jail for his courageous article on the disgusting Regent of Great Britain, who later became known as George IV, he papered his cell with rose-patterned wallpaper! He arranged his own "inscape." Many people have created their own inner scenery with faith and hope, dark without, but light within. The words of St. Paul cover the possibilities: "Though our outward man is decaying, the inward man is being renewed day by day."

One great gift of the gospel is that of a bright and radiant inner light. A person is poorly prepared for the contingencies of life who is wholly dependent on the attractiveness of the outer landscape, the external environment of life. This may quickly and unexpectedly change. Money may vanish, position may slip, health may give way.

If these outward things are all one has to depend on, if he has no "inscape" which will remain unchanged, even when the outward landscape changes, he is poor indeed. "Be strengthened with might through his Spirit in the inner man."

38 ❋ "You Look Like a Million Dollars"

STOP, LOOK and listen for a moment to the words above. We hear them nearly every day. And they are good words, for they convey a hearty, friendly greeting. They mean, "You look wonderful." There is no snarl in them. Just a tribute.

But how strange and disturbing it is that our highest tribute to a person is to compare him to a pile of money! It seems like an unintended indication that our highest measurement is a financial one. We never say, "You look like a sunrise," or "You look like a rainbow." Yet these are more beautiful than a million dollars.

In comparison, we recall the words of a soldier in the terrible hospital at Scutari in the Crimean War. When Florence Nightingale came into that place, the soldier said, "You look like the grace of God." He was right. She was part of the grace of God, love acting through skill for the saving of life.

The poet has a truer conception of the worth of things. Burns did not write, "My love is like a million pounds." If he had, no one would ever have sung the song. He wrote:

> O my luv's like a red, red rose
> That's newly spring in June;
> Oh, my luve's like the melodie
> That's sweetly play'd in tune.

William Blake has asked the question in another form: "What, it will be questioned, when the sun rises, do you not see a round disk of fire, somewhat like a guinea? 'Oh, no, no, I see an innumerable company of the heavenly host crying, "Holy, Holy, Holy, is the lord God Almighty!" ' "

Which do we see most clearly, a coin, or a heavenly host?

75

39 ❖ The 100 Most Important People

I T WILL come as a surprise to most people to learn that there is a paper-bound book, published by Pocket Books entitled *The 100 Most Important People in the World Today*. The publishers say that the list of people will be changed as the years go by.

The whole idea is a piece of monstrous impertinence. Who is competent to list the 100 most important people now living? What scales would be the right ones on which to weigh people? If we go back into history, we learn that no one can ever tell on any day who might be the most important person. Try it. Think of the date, February 12, 1809. Most anyone would have said that on that day the most important person was Napoleon, then at the height of his power. They would have been all wrong. The most important person, as seen 150 years later, was undoubtedly a baby, a few hours old, born in a one-room log cabin on the frontier of Kentucky, Abraham Lincoln! So today, no doubt the most important person living again may be a baby, a few hours old, born in a hospital, farmhouse, or tenement. Remember, that was true of the world about 4 B.C.—the most important person was a Baby, born in a barn.

Great events and great persons have a way of coming on quiet feet.

Suppose, in all reverence, God made up a list of the "100 Most Important People." Who would be on it? All we can say is that if there were such a list (we know that the very idea is foolish, for "all service ranks the same with God"), we would all be terribly surprised.

We have one clue to God's order of importance. It is found in the unnoticed people to whom Jesus gave his praise. Three times, at least, he picked out people for honorable mention, and in each case they were people whom others standing by, including his own disciples, did not notice at all. One was a Roman Centurion, of a class of people whom the Jews heartily despised. Jesus made it clear that the man was truly great, for he said: "I have not found such faith in all

76

Israel." A second person was a poor widow, putting two small coins into the almsbox. Jesus stopped and awarded her a Distinguished Service Medal, in his words: "She has put in more than them all." In his eyes, she was one of the truly important people in Jerusalem. It was so with a third person. She broke an alabaster box of very valuable perfume out of love of him. She did not count the cost. Jesus said of her that she would have an everlasting memorial in the minds of men. She was a Very Important Person.

There is a book, in which there is a list of people, which counts far more than any *Who's Who in America*, or *The Social Register*, or this little book, *The* 100 *Most Important People in the World Today*. It is called in the Bible, *The Lamb's Book of Life*.

40 ✿ The Church Belongs to Me

THERE IS a picturesque remark, worth much thought, in the recent biography of a notorious, lusty Texas character in the wild early days of Texas, a man called Shanghai Pierce. The author, Chris Emmet, relates that on the 200,000 acre ranch, which Shanghai Pierce owned, he decided to "introduce religion" and built a small church. A visitor asked Mr. Pierce: "Do you belong to this church?" Mr. Pierce answered, violently: "Hell no! It belongs to me."

Think that over, without the profanity! It was a true statement. The big rancher did not belong to the church. It belonged to him! There is an immeasurable distance between the two. Which statement most truly applies to us? Do we belong to the Church or does "our" church belong to us?

There is a common way of saying "my church" which expresses exactly this relationship; a kind of proprietorship; something we use like "my house" or "my car." It is one of the pleasant appendages of life, on a level with "my golf club."

This, however, is not the New Testament use of the word Church, the "body of Christ." If we truly belong to the Church, instead of its "belonging" to us, its gospel will dominate us, it will have the right of way in our lives, and we will be a real and vital part of all its efforts to hasten the Kingdom of God on earth.

41 ✤ 113 by 26

THE FIGURES above look like a puzzle or a set of magic numbers. They are both. They represent one of the great puzzles of history. They have worked real magic.

Not to be too mysterious about it, those figures represent the dimensions, length and breadth, of the *Mayflower,* the ship which brought the Pilgrims to America in 1620. The measurements in feet look pitifully small. How could a crate like that amount to anything? If we could see it, or a life-sized model of it, we would wonder if such a "rowboat" could sail around Manhattan Island. But it did sail into history!

This little ship emphasizes the point powerfully that size ought never to be confused with significance. It is not the size of anything which makes it important, but the use to which it is put. Measured by horsepower, the *Queen Elizabeth* is a much greater ship than the *Mayflower.* Beside the *Queen Elizabeth,* with her hundreds of passengers, many of them famous, the queer little *Mayflower,* with its prosaic company of middle-class tradesmen, makes a poor showing. The *Mayflower* could be carried on the deck of the *Queen Elizabeth* without displacing even a shuffleboard game. There was very little show about the *Mayflower.* But there was power! In the spiritual ideal and iron will of men and women in the little company, there was power enough to create a Christian civilization—a new world.

Such a remembrance should bring hope and a new morale to a person who thinks he is placed in a 2 by 4 situation. He might think, "I could do something if I had a real opportunity, but what can done in this dump?" Remember that something else was small, a little ship 113 by 26! Those are good numbers to repeat.

42 ❀ A Message from Mars

IT IS no wonder that the Man from Mars has been one of the most overworked figures of literature and journalism. The idea of a stranger to our planet looking us over and giving his opinions about the way we do things, gives a wonderful opportunity for social and economic criticism.

One such comment, well deserving remembrance, is that of Don Marquis, who imagined this message coming through from the planet Mars, after communication had been established in the far future:

We are creatures inhabiting a planet which is inhabited by creatures who cannot agree what they are or where they came from, or where they are going to; but we are on our way.

Earth flashes back the message—"Same here."

That imagined exchange of messages has at least the virtue of raising the biggest questions of human life: What are we? Where did we come from? Where are we going? All the major questions of destiny are wrapped up in those three queries. When those questions are not raised, life becomes trivial and mean, and heads for disaster both for individuals and for society.

It is the task of Christianity to give convincing answers to those fundamental questions. Nowhere is there found in such small space such complete answers as in the passage in the 13th chapter of the Gospel of St. John, which records the story of Jesus' washing the disciples' feet: "Jesus . . . knowing that he had come from God and was going to God, rose from supper, laid aside his garments, and girded himself with a towel."

There we have it—knowing that his origin was in God, and that his destiny was God, he could stoop to take upon himself the lowliest duties of service to men. There we have the Christian answers to these great questions.

Who are we? We are children of God; our origin is in Him. Where are we going? To "God who is our Home."

43 ✿ *Penurious Living*

A HARDY PERENNIAL among newspaper stories—hardly a month goes by without some variant of it appearing somewhere—is that of a person found in conditions of dire poverty, near starvation, or dead of starvation, with a large amount of cash or bonds, or both, in a trunk somewhere in the room, or a bankbook showing the possession of thousands of dollars. Miserliness is a very queer quirk of human nature.

But that is not the only kind of penurious living on great wealth. It is a much more common thing than it ought to be in the religious life of people, this living penuriously while the great wealth of the grace of God is available for them.

Here, in classic words, are the assets of the Christian for daily living: "Now to him who by the power at work within us is able to do far more abundantly than all we ask or think." That is the bank balance, and it is a tremendous one.

Yet how little of it we draw out. Instead of living by that wealth of grace, so many subsist miserably on fears and hesitations, far below the spiritual poverty line. It is as though a person with a million dollars in the bank should live on $3.75 a week.

One reason for this abject poverty in the midst of possible wealth is that God does not become or remain a real factor or possession in life. He becomes a God whose being they no longer feel, and whose presence they have long forgotten. Dr. C. A. Briggs, in his commentary on the Psalms, makes this acute observation:

In the 14th Psalm we read of fools or impious men who say in their hearts, "There is no God." But it is God's effective presence rather than His existence that is being denied, so that we should perhaps translate, "No God is here."

That is the frequent cause of penurious spiritual living. People say,

82

"No God is here," in the midst of their daily life, and as far as they are concerned that is equivalent to saying, "There is no God."

Such persons never experience the surplus living there is pictured in the statement: "In Him there is fullness of joy." Their measure of joy is marginal, to say the least. They never have the proof of the promise: "In His service there is great reward." They are so miserly with their strength that they never serve enough to have any great reward.

There is an old song that fits this need: "Out of my want, and into Thy wealth."

44 ✿ *A Knock at the Door*

HERE IS a word from Charles Lamb to which everyone will respond and say: "That is absolutely true."

Not many sounds in life, and I include all urban and rural sounds, exceed in interest a knock at the door.

We all know from our own experience that it is true. Sometimes it has been tragically true. Under totalitarian rule, in Germany and in Italy and in Russia, an unexpected knock at the door has often meant the swift coming of the secret police, and imprisonment and death. To multitudes of helpless people, that knock has been the very crack of doom. Someone has said with graphic truth that the mark of a free country is that, when you hear a noise in the hall, or a knock at the door, you know it is the milkman, and not the Gestapo!

One of the most impressive scenes in all the plays of Shakespeare is the knocking at the gate in Macbeth, after the murder has been committed. It sounds like the coming of doom. It is. It dramatizes the breaking in of conscience and consequences, the breaking in of the eternal into time.

This observation of Charles Lamb's throws a light on the word of Jesus: "Behold, I stand at the door and knock." Nothing in life approaches in importance Christ's knock on our door.

Christ knocks at the door of life when it unfolds, when one looks out on the years and considers life's possibilities. He says, "Let me in. Let me be a part of your life, your guide, your friend, your master." That is the great red-letter day of your life, when one answers that knock and says: "Come in, Lord."

Christ knocks at our door with opportunity. He knocks to call us out of our little rooms into wide fields of service. "The Master is come and calleth for Thee." When he knocks, with his summons to

84

be a fellow workman with God, do not hang up the sign "Busy," or "Not at home."

Christ knocks at the doors of grief. He comes into dark rooms as well as into brightly lighted ones. We read in the Gospel of John: "And Jesus came, the doors being shut." Often doors of grief are tightly shut, so tight that there seems to be no chance of there ever being any sunlight again. If we will open, he will come in, even to the darkest gloom, and we can hear him say, convincingly: "Be of good cheer. I am the resurrection and the life."

45 ✿ Is God on Your Christmas List?

AN UNFORGETTABLE part of the Christmas story in the gospel of Matthew is the record of the first Christmas gifts. When the Wise Men found the Christ Child, they opened their treasure and gave gifts. The first Christmas gifts were given to Christ. So often today, people give gifts to each other, but give nothing to Christ, nothing to God.

What kind of Christmas gift would be suitable to give to God? It is a principle of wise giving that the gift be something that can be used. You do not give your grandmother a pair of roller skates, unless she is an unusual grandmother. You do not give young George, aged nine years, a set of the *Encyclopaedia Britannica*, bound in leather. A Christmas gift to God must be something He can use. God does not want and cannot use merely good wishes in the costly enterprise of overcoming evil and bringing in a kingdom of righteousness, joy, and peace. He cannot use a person's easy, sentimental admiration for Jesus. Mere words, no matter how beautiful, are no acceptable gift to God.

The gift of your *mind*—that would be a gift God wants and can use. To allow your ideas to be formed by the mind of Jesus; to love what he loved; to hate what he hated; to restrain your insistent desires by bringing them into captivity to his spirit, that would be a genuine celebration of Christmas. Then to give God your *strength*—to add the impact of your life to the force of the peacemakers of the earth; to refuse to accept our present world as the best possible, and daringly to work for a more Christian order of life—that will be the equivalent of the gold, frankincense, and myrrh of the Wise Men.

46 ✿ *The Rescue of Jesus*

IT IS AN axiom of history that every great figure needs, from time to time, to be rescued from the accumulations that have gathered around him and have come to obscure his real nature. Take Shakespeare, for instance. Often compulsory study of his plays in school has made him appear to be a bore to young people, and the great master of drama is buried out of sight. One of the finest actors of our day, Maurice Evans, has recently written of Ivor Brown's book, *Shakespeare:*

What is refreshingly different in his approach is that, unlike so many of his more pedagogic predecessors, he sets out to rescue his hero from the library and the classroom and restore him to the stage for which he wrote and on which he acted.

A rescue expedition vastly needed!

Or take George Washington. The man has been lost in the stone statue which has been made out of him. Recently Dr. Douglas S. Freeman has led a rescue expedition in his notable four-volume life of Washington, and the Father of his Country has emerged as more of a man and less of a statue.

Much has been written in late years of "the problem of Jesus," in which he is a highly controversial figure. That is necessary, for there is need to learn all that we can about Jesus from scholarship. Yet that has shut from the eyes of many the first great fact about Jesus, which is that he is not primarily a problem, but an answer, God's answer to man's need. Richard Watson Gilder has pictured such a "rescue" that each of us needs continually to make, to get Jesus out of the library into the life:

Behold Him now as He comes!
Not the Christ of our subtle creeds,

But the Light of our hearts and homes,
Our hopes, our fears, our needs.

Jesus needs to be rescued in our thinking and acting from being merely a statue, venerated but away from life. As in the old Greek fable, the statue must come to life.

The Crusades in the Middle Ages were expeditions to rescue the tomb of Jesus from the Mohammedans. There is a far nobler crusade in our day, to rescue, not the tomb of Jesus, but the Master himself, out of the prisons in which his full, great meaning has been concealed.

O Master, from the mountain's side

O tread the city's streets again.

47 ❉ In Debt to Palestine

M D. C. CRAWFORD in his book, *The Conquest of Culture*, tells an interesting detail of our debt to Egypt. Here is some of the debt we owe:

When I get out of bed I have paid Egypt a compliment in two respects. In the first place, the idea of a bed was first conceived by a Nile craftsman. Second, time was the invention of an Egyptian mathematician. My sheets, being of cotton, I can date at least at 3000 B.C. . . . Ram's head seals and a lamb stew found in a covered earthen pot at Tel Asmar imply a date for wool in my blanket. And as I dress I reflect that my tailored suit was sewn with a needle, which invention belongs to the earliest civilization in Egypt.

So much for Egypt. Now come to a larger debt—the debt we owe to Palestine. H. G. Wells once made the dogmatic judgment: "Nothing important happened in Palestine." That calls for a resounding "Is that so?" A sermon might well undertake to state, as concisely and effectively as can be done in half an hour, the debt that every man living owes to Palestine and to those who lived and labored there. It is a debt far greater than the one we owe to Egypt for cotton and wool, for glass and time measurement, or the one we owe to Phoenicia for sailing vessels.

Take the life of an inhabitant of an American city for a week, and trace the debt he owes at every step to the Hebrew and Christian revelation. Our courts, schools, libraries—what would they be without the shaping influence of Christianity? Our homes—what would they be, without the inheritance from Palestine, as traced in the Bible and its influence? Or our churches? More than that, in these days approaching despair on the part of multitudes, what would be our hope of individual or social salvation, were it not for what has come out of Palestine, and supremely, for Him who culminated the gifts of Palestine, Jesus?

A newspaper had this headline to a feature article last year—"Palestine still in the News." It is, truly. The "good news" still comes from Palestine.

48 ❖ *Cut Off from the Past*

THERE IS an arresting text in *Acts* which describes the
Athenians, who "spent their time in nothing except telling
and hearing something new." (*Acts* 17:21) How well this
text applies to a prevalent mood of our time! Such prestige is at-
tached to the new that hosts of people are being cut off from the past.
There is disdain for the old; it has no value for people who desire
above all things to be "up to date." A five-year-old-girl asked her
twenty-seven-year-old mother: "Did you wear hoop skirts in the old
days, mamma?" To her, evidently, anyone older than six or seven
lived in "the old days." So it is with many who have succumbed to the
blight of contemporaneousness.

The circumstances of city life generally induce this disregard for
the past. With the increased speed of change of every sort and the
rapid movement of population, the average city dweller tends to be
cut off from his own past. The French have a word for it, *déraciné*.
It is hard to visualize a past when you have not lived in it. How
many city people know where their great-grandparents are buried?
Or their grandparents, for that matter?

The great tragedy of our time, its wars and waste, is due largely
to its isolation from the great past of the Christian revelation, the
truths that would have saved the world. One of our great spiritual
gains is the recovery from the past by Christian theology of the faith
that God revealed Himself in Christ, which is an older and deeper
view than the brisk, optimistic confidence so often mistaken for Christian faith.

Our era is emphatically an age of discovery. The greatest and most
needed discovery must come from the Christian past—the realization
of the deed of God in Christ, which is the only hope for the redemption of the world. A "rootless generation"—an apt description
of so many people in our day—must be rooted and grounded in
faith.

91

49 ✳ The Royal Road to Romance

SOME READERS will recognize the words above as the title of one of Richard Halliburton's books of travel. He always wrote with gusto and a certain boyishness, reflecting his unfailing amazement at the marvelous world and the excitement of romance.

The words might truly be the title of an Easter meditation, for the Easter truth is the Royal Road to Romance.

In recent years, that word "romance' has gone under a cloud. It has been regarded as the opposite to "realism," and today most people are all for realism. Romance is a rosy view of things, beautiful, perhaps, but not true. It is considered an illusion, or wishful thinking. We do not wish to call a man a liar, so we call him a "romantic optimist," which is about the same thing.

But the dictionary has another meaning for "romance": "that which heightens and colors the commonplace quality of life." That is exactly the sense in which the Christian gospel is the Royal Road to Romance. It heightens and colors the commonplace quality of life. So, Easter is the high and true romance of man's life.

Think of the heightening and coloring of existence which come from the Easter revelation that personality is the supreme thing in the universe. We get a glimpse of it in Emerson's phrase, "Man's enchanted dust." Man is made of the dust of the ground. But it is "enchanted dust," for man is a child of God, who will never in all eternity be lost to his Father's love. That is the true romance which makes all the fairy stories ever written seem as dull as a telephone directory.

Evelyn Underhill writes that Francis of Assisi "ran away to God, some boys ran away to sea." It was a great adventure. In fact, it was the Royal Road to Romance.

Another aspect of the Royal Road is found in one of the profoundly religious passages in modern English literature. It is in Masefield's long poem, "The Widow in the Bye Street," where a brokenhearted mother is making a last prayer for her son, who is to be executed for murder. She prays:

> And God who gave his mercies, takes his mercies,
> And God who gives beginnings, gives the end.
> A rest for broken things too broke to mend.[1]

Think of that last line—"broken things too broke to mend." Life has many broken things "too broke to mend," diseases from which one cannot recover, losses which one can never forget, disappointments too great to be passed over, failures too complete ever to be made over. Easter comes into life and proclaims that all broken things are still in the hands of the Mender of broken earthenware, and eternal life comes with its powers beyond earthly resources.

[1] From *Collected Poems* by John Masefield. Used by permission of The Macmillan Company.

50 ✿ *Something for Nothing*

A WOMAN was recently describing a fairly familiar sight in the New York subway, and anywhere else where vending machines for chewing gum and candy are placed. She saw a small boy go the whole length of the subway station platform, pushing in the plungers of all the slot machines, a dozen of them. He had not put in any coin. He just hoped that by some miracle he might get a piece of gum or candy without putting in any coin. Perhaps someone put in a penny and forgot to push the plunger.

It was a very good picture of the effort many people make to get something for nothing. As the little boy went along the subway platform, so they have gone through life, making futile efforts to get something for nothing, to take out some prize without putting in any effort. A person will say what he will do "when my ship comes in," forgetting the fact that he has never sent any ship out to sea.

We do not expect such fantastic result in our finances. We do not look for the postman to bring us a quarterly dividend from General Motors if we have not bought any stock. But in other realms people do indulge in such futile expectations.

Take *friendship*, for instance. It is common to hear people complain that they are neglected and lonely, that a callous world passes them by and that they are condemned to isolation. Often the reason is that they have tried to take something out without putting anything in. They have wanted to *have* friends but have never tried to *be* friends. They have made no costly investment in care and concern for others, and they get nothing out of the slot machine into which they have put no coin.

It is true of the *religious life*. Jesus said that the measure we give is the measure we receive. Some people complain that they do not "get much" out of their religion, that prayer does not do much for

94

them, that they do not have the joy that they read about. They have never put enough into it to get much out.

So with the *larger social issues*. Many people, for instance, would like to have world peace drop into the world's lap. They do not realize that so costly a thing as peace comes with a high price. Jesus in the Beatitudes said: "Blessed are the *peacemakers*"—not "Blessed are the *peace-wishers*." It is the makers, the people who put in an investment of sacrificial toil and life, who can look forward to winning the prize of peace. So it is with every other socially desirable result.

How much are we putting in?

51 ❖ Deficiency Diseases

PRESENT-DAY MEDICINE has a term used much more than it was a generation ago, or even five years ago. It is "deficiency diseases." In recent years medicine has made marvelous strides along two main lines. It has wrought miracles in combating microbes and non-filterable viruses which attack the body, its organs, and cells. Such powerful reliances in the fight for life as the whole sulpha family of drugs, streptomycin, and others have reduced the death rate enormously. The other great line of advance has been in remedying deficiencies in the human body. There are ills due, not so much to infection, as to lack of necessary ingredients in the body. Vitamins and other aids have helped in this advance. Some forms of thyroid and ills of basal metabolism are forms of "deficiency diseases."

It is a short jump from thinking of deficiency diseases in the body to the same thing in the spiritual life. That is, there are grievous ills which are due, not so much to infection by evil, deliberate acts of sin, as to the lack of forces which make for health and strength of the soul and of the church. These are dangerous shortages.

We get a glimpse of one in the words of Jesus: "When the Son of Man comes, will he find faith on the earth?" That is one great deficiency disease—*too little faith*, too little of downright belief in Jesus Christ. The excuse often given is: "Well, of course, we mustn't be ridiculous." The answer to that is: "Why not?" For that is what the first heralds of the cross who went out into the Roman and Greek world were, in the sight of the wise and mighty of their time. They were "ridiculous." They were small; they were weak; but they had a faith that God would use them, so that the kingdoms of this world should become "the kingdom of our God and of His Christ." Ridiculous! Or was it? It is faith that will keep life erect against evils, that will keep the church moving against wrong, that will not be overwhelmed by forces making for war.

There is often a deficiency of *out-thrust*, not enough reaching out to carry the truth to men and women and children. Too many of us are content to be "sitting pretty." If so, we are sitting, all right, but not very "pretty." Too much sitting together in heavenly places; not enough standing together in unheavenly places.

Part of the trouble is a *deficiency of knowledge* of our own faith. We have it in scraps. We do not have a steady enough renewal of knowledge. So many often, in a crisis, do not know "whose they are." The poet Edward Arlington Robinson has described this lack movingly:

> We know the truth that has been
> told to the world a thousand times,
> But we have no ears to listen yet
> to more than fragments of it; we have heard
> a murmur, now and then; an echo, here
> And there . . .

A murmur and an echo are not enough.

The soul as well as the body needs new invigorators, new stamina, new energy, from our God who has much to give, above all that we can ask or think.

52 ❀ Look!

A VERY COMMON expression in our world where there is so much to see is "Look!"

There is a striking use of it in the story of Palm Sunday, where, after the triumphal entry, Mark describes Jesus and his disciples going about the city of Jerusalem, looking at all things. When they came to the Temple, the disciples exclaimed: "Look, Teacher, what wonderful stones and what wonderful buildings." It was a perfectly natural feeling for country men from Galilee gazing at the wonders of the big city. Jesus also said "Look," but his gaze was directed at a sight very different. A poor widow, whose self-sacrificing gift was dropped into the alms box, was far more wonderful than any stones. Jesus was interested in *quality* of life, not in *quantity* of material. He weighed the Temple as an institution on religious and ethical balances, and found it wanting. Because it failed to meet these tests, he said that not one stone would be left on another.

This word of Jesus in the Temple comes as a sharp rebuke to a quantitative civilization, as ours is so largely, full of mechanical wonders and miraculous gadgets of every sort. Men have an awe before bigness that partakes of the nature of worship. In estimating our society they cry: "Look!" Look at the airplanes, at the total of bank clearings, at the freight car loadings, and all the other measures of progress and prosperity. Jesus says: "Look!"—not at the size, but the ethical and spiritual quality of our life and civilization. On those scales all of our bigness must be weighed.

We ought not to forget, also, that these words of Jesus were spoken in the Temple in judgment on a religious institution. Jesus still brings to his church the measure of quality rather than quantity. We may say: "Look, Master, at this church; what wonderful buildings. St.

98

Croesus' Church, with floor space almost equal to that of the railroad station." He is not impressed. As on that day in the Temple, his eye will wander off in search of other things, such as evidence of inner life and devotion to God's kingdom.

53 ✿ Stalemate

THERE IS a very arresting sentence in Sir Winston Churchill's volume on World War II, entitled *The Hinge of Fate*. He is describing the situation as it was changing from defeat to hope or the allied powers in 1943. He wrote, "Between victory and urvival there are many stages. Henceforth our danger was not detruction but stalemate."

That is a great danger in many realms of effort. Stalemate means deadlock, a standstill where nothing moves. It is true of the Christian Church. Its danger is not that of betrayal by its members. Not many of the run-of-the mill members of the Church would renounce their faith if they were subjected to some dramatic test. There have been many martyrs who have laid down their lives in the past ten years. The real danger is what Sir Winston feared for the allied forces, slowing down to a standstill. The Church of Laodicea in the Book of Revelation achieved a stalemate. It was neutral, all animation gone, neither hot nor cold—only fit for spewing.

So today the Church may be engulfed in such a flood of sweet reasonableness that it comes to a standstill. There are different hazards of life which bring on a stalemate. For one thing, the message grows stale. People have heard it over and over. It makes no more permanent impression than hail on a slate roof. It does not pierce to the central places of the mind and heart. If we do not allow the message to become real, it passes over us.

One of the most important things to remember is this: that no doctrine can live in the intellect if it does not renew itself in experience. If it does not renew itself in experience, it becomes just words. How can the doctrine that God hears prayer mean anything if it is not renewed in the experience of praying? How can the words "take up your cross" have any power over us at all if we do not have the experience of doing it?

The second danger is that of the defense complex. We have churches which make their great goal holding their own. The tennis player, Mr. Tilden, said that the sign of old age in a sportsman was playing a defensive game. And it is the sign of old age in the churches. If a church has no concern but holding its own, has no desire for new adventure, the death rattle is already in its throat.

54 ✢ "I Saw Also the Lord"

THERE IS a big little word in one of the great chapters of the Bible, the sixth chapter of Isaiah. The first verse reads, in the King James Version: "In the year that King Uzziah died, I saw also the Lord." Notice the *also*. A truly large word, standing for the double vision Christians so deeply need—realism plus faith. Isaiah looked out on his time and saw all the gloomy facts there were to see, the loss of the King, the turmoil and confusion, the national danger and sinfulness of his people. He did not turn a blind eye to a single calamity. But he saw more than that. He saw *also* the Lord. In the midst of all the uncertainty and adversity, there was something else to see: "The Lord, high and lifted up." God was the biggest factor in the situation.

It is a needed word for today. There is nothing to be gained and everything to be lost by taking a superficial, optimistic, and unreal view of great difficulties. The classic example of that mistake is the Roman Pliny, who refused to try to escape from Pompeii when the eruption of Mt. Vesuvius buried the whole area. He replied blandly, "Everything will be all right." It wasn't. He was buried under the flow of lava.

We see clearly the tragedies and catastrophes of our time and world. We need to see *also* the Lord. We need for our support the vision of faith that His Kingdom is an everlasting Kingdom. We need the clear eyes of faith that enabled one to say, in a time of darkness centuries ago: "The church of God is not a candle, Blow on!"

55 ✿ *Three Classes of People*

SOMEONE HAS said that there are three classes of people: those who *make* things happen; those who *watch* things happen; and the overwhelming majority who have *no idea of what is happening.*

Think it over. It is roughly true of any era of history. It was true in the first Christian century. There were a devoted few who were making things happen in the Roman Empire. They were bringing the Gospel of Christ into the Roman world, and a vast change was beginning to take place, a new spiritual climate was being brought in. There were many who merely watched it. And there was the majority who had no idea of what was going on.

It was true also of the Puritan migration to America. There was a devoted and intrepid group who were *making* things happen. They were laying the foundation of a new nation. Others were merely watching. The majority in England in 1620 had no idea that anything important was going on.

Isn't it true also in any local church? There is the group, sometimes small, who make things happen, who lead the church into real service. There are those who watch, often sympathetically, but who are still bystanders. And there is a larger fringe who really know nothing of what is being attempted or done.

One of the finest Promotion Days that ever come to a person is when he is promoted from the second or third group into the first. In the struggle for world peace and survival, we can be among those who make things happen. None of us will ever be Secretary of State or General of the Army. But we may each be a vital part of the ultimate power in a democracy—public opinion.

56 ❖ Adventures with Discarded Materials

HERE IS a book which many a housewife might play around with, and have the time of her life. Its title is, *Art Adventures with Discarded Materials*, by Evadna Kraus Perry. The title itself is enough to start a treasure hunt in cellar and attic. (Perhaps the man in the house will want to include the hard sofa in the living room under the heading of "discarded materials"!)

The book tells how to make art creations out of such unpromising materials as old newspapers, rags, tin cans, gunny sacks, and flower sacks. We have not seen any of the "creations." They may not rival Michelangelo's statue of Moses. But the book promises exciting adventure.

The subtitle catches the imagination, and describes far more than making artistic things out of scraps. It is, "In the trash box lie thrilling adventures."

In that sentence there is great history. Great achievements have come from people who were regarded as "discarded materials" by many in their time. Paderewski was told to give up all hopes of becoming a pianist when he was given an audition by a celebrated teacher. He was told that since he had a large upper lip, he might find a place as a cornet player in a band! Lincoln was regarded by many of his contemporaries, until his election as President, as an unpromising man, who had often been defeated for office. George Washington Carver was a former slave.

It has been the glory of the Christian religion that it has created beauty and power from men who seemed to be in the "trash box" of human life; men such as Jerry McCauley and John B. Gough, who were lifted out of the gutter of drink, to become powerful forces for good. Again and again, "the stone which the builders rejected has become the head of the corner."

But this is all more than history. It is a picture of the possibilities of our own lives. We too can have "adventures in discarded materials," in our dealings with people. If we can look on people with the eyes of faith, and put ourselves to the task of bringing out those possibilities, we can have a share in the creation of the person they may become. That has been done in innumerable instances by the faithful work of a teacher. A class of unruly boys has seemed to be an unpromising trash can of human nature, a terrible headache for the teacher. The question has been asked, "Can any good come out of a gang like that?" To that many have said an emphatic "No!" But there have been others who have seen in that tough group of boys a challenge and an opportunity for personal investment of love, faith, patience, and help, and they have had truly exciting "adventures with discarded materials." They have helped to shape and guide boys into strong Christian manhood.

57 ✿ Explorer

A VISITOR IN a home, confronted with a bright six-year-old boy, began the unavoidable "interview" with the usual question, "What are you going to be when you grow up?" The boy did not hesitate for an instant. "I am going to be an explorer," he replied, firmly and finally.

He had picked out a vocation with great and alluring attractions, and a strong appeal to youth. To be sure, the boy's horizons had already been extended.

The familiar painting, "The Youth of Sir Walter Raleigh," is a most vivid picture of the lure of exploration. An old sailor, seated on the side of a weather-beaten dory, is telling a tall tale to the young boy, Raleigh, who is looking up into his face, spellbound, with eyes glistening at the mystery and wonder of faraway places.

That lure, strong in youth, can last a lifetime. In Tennyson's "Ulysses," there is the classic picture of the appeal of the distant horizon, even to old age:

> Come, my friends,
> 'Tis not too late to seek a newer world
> For my purpose holds,
> To sail beyond the sunset and the paths
> Of all the western stars, until I die.

The role of the explorer is a fascinating one in every sort of life. The vocation of the explorer is not unlike the vocation of the Christian disciple. If he follows his high calling, he is an explorer of the mysteries of the world, and of the possibilities of life, making inward and outward discoveries.

There is, first of all, *the exploration of ourselves.* This is a field for discovery: What is the meaning of the self, this bewildering

106

entanglement of desires, capacities, appetites and yearnings? There are many people who have never discovered that country. They may have made the journey around the world but have never made a journey around their skull! The striking fact is that the continents of America were discovered before the circulation of the blood was discovered. The outward exploration preceded the inward one. Man is more than the bundle of appetites which he shares with any cocker spaniel. Walt Whitman gives an invitation to inward discovery in his words: "There is more to me than is contained between my hat and my shoes." Make a journey of exploration until we discover the child of God within us.

Second, there is the supreme exploration which *leads to the discovery of God*. The Psalms state this truth unforgettably: "My heart and my flesh cry out for the living God . . . As the heart panteth for the water brooks, so my heart panteth for Thee, O God." St. Augustine puts it: "Thou hast made us for thyself." God is "the last home of mystery." This search dwarfs every other undertaking. Gamaliel Bradford is not far from human experience, when he gives his own experience:

> But my one unchanged obsession,
> Where so e'er my feet have trod,
> Is a keen, enormous, haunting,
> Never-sated thirst for God.

Third, *exploration in human relations* is a first necessity today. Men must discover better ways of living together; for if they do not, the only thing left will be ways of dying together. Men did find better ways of lifting burdens than on their own backs. They discovered steam and electricity. They must find better ways of contact with one another than by means of guns and bombs; ways of cooperation rather than exploitation.

Fourth, the last voyage is the *alluring expedition into eternity*. We will all make that some time. Death is not a dead end. It is the beginning of a voyage.

Tennyson pictures the last great explorer's trip:

Sunset and evening star
And one clear call for me;
And may there be no moaning of the bar
When I put out to sea.

58 ❊ Dire Poverty

MANY YEARS ago Rudyard Kipling made a commencement address at McGill University in Montreal. He said one striking thing which deserves to be kept in remembrance. He was warning the students against an overconcern for money, or position, or glory. He said: "Some day you will meet a man who cares for none of these things. Then you will know how poor you are."

That has happened on a grand scale. Jesus cared for none of these things. And for nineteen centuries he has led many people to see how poor they are with only a collection of *things* to show for their journey through life, and no spiritual resources. Three contrasts will lead us into the theme, by giving concrete proof of the truth which Kipling declared. Contrast Pilate with the prisoner before him, Jesus. Pilate was deeply concerned with position and power. Jesus cared for none of these things. Which was the richer in all that makes a great personality and true success in life? Contrast Nero, the Roman Emperor, and the prisoner named Paul who was beheaded in Nero's reign. Who was the real pauper, Nero or Paul?

Drop down to the nineteenth century. Beyond question the two most notable figures in the history of Africa in the nineteenth century were Cecil Rhodes and David Livingstone. Rhodes amassed millions exploiting South Africa, with its gold and its diamonds. His desire to seize all of South Africa for the British Empire was one of the chief causes of the Boer War. Rhodes died worth many millions of dollars. The other figure was a missionary and explorer, Livingstone. He gave his life not only to bring the gospel of Christ to the black people of Central Africa, but also to fight against slavery and all the oppressions with which they were beset. He died with hardly a cent to his name. But his grave in Westminster Abbey is one of the great shrines of the world. When we look at Livingstone who cared for none of these prizes that make life a fitful fever for so many, we see how poor Cecil Rhodes really was.

59 ❖ *Noise and Fog*

THE ENGLISH poet, Stephen Spender, has made an impressive picture of the truth so much stressed in the Gospel, that of the necessity of renewal of spirit and of soul. Here are his words:

> Swear, never to allow
> Gradually to smother,
> With noise and fog,
> The flowering of the spirit.

Notice the keen observation of the poet in singling out the two things so destructive of the life of the soul—noise and fog. Those are two things against which we must continually struggle if we are to keep "the life of God in the soul of man." Those two forces are particularly active in our day.

Consider *noise*. We live in a bath of noise. It keeps breaking in all the time, through the radio, traffic noise, telephone, pneumatic drills. We all remember Edgar Allan Poe's poem "The Bells," in which he experiments with words giving the effect of clanging bells. The last line of each stanza is "Bells, bells, bells, bells." Today we could write a more clanging poem than Poe did, for we know more about disturbing bells; we hear more of them—doorbells, telephone bells, alarm clocks, "bells, bells, bells, bells." Poe never knew the half of it!

If the soul is to have the quiet necessary for its preservation from smothering, that quiet must be deliberately made. It never just happens, not in our noise-filled world. We must deliberately create the present-day fulfillment of the words of Jesus: "Enter into thy closet, and shut the door."

Consider *fog*. Fog, as every seaman knows, can be a terribly dangerous thing. Fog over the mind can be just as fatal. When the moral and spiritual lighthouses and buoys marking a true course go into low visibility or complete disappearance, the shipwreck of life

111

is imminent. So many people today are enveloped by fog. That is, there are no great imperatives in their lives; nothing stands out clearly as the way to be taken. And, as Mr. Spender points out, "the flowering of the spirit" is smothered. To avoid fog we need light by which we may see clearly the things that matter most. We need the light of him who is the Light of the World.

60 ❖ "For an Easier Key"

A MAN SAID to his wife after attending Sunday morning service not long ago: "I got quite a kick out of the hymnbook this morning." His wife looked shocked.

"Is that what you go to church for?" she said.

"Oh," he protested, "not while the sermon was going on, or the prayers, but during the anthem. I was looking at the musical directions at the top of a number of the hymns, and one startled me. It was the hymn, 'O Mind of God.' At the top it said: 'For an easier key, see #366.' I said to myself, 'That is what we are always doing— trying to put the great music of the Gospel into an easier key.'"

He had something there. Take the first stanza of that hymn: "O mind of God, broad as the sky. . . ." Oh, we say, not that broad please. Let's put it into an easier key. That is awfully broad. It includes everybody. There is no allowance for my pet prejudices and my limitations. One of the tragedies of the world today is that we try to sing the breadth of the loving God in an easier key, which leaves out many of His children.

Or take the second stanza: "O heart of God, deep as the needs of all humanity." Again we say, let's not make it that deep. That would hurt. Let's try something a bit easier. Not the needs of all humanity, but the needs of my own family, my own group. There are too many needs in the world. It makes a person dizzy. Let's forget that. If we take that into our hearts, it will spoil everything. So we try an easier key.

The third stanza starts: "O will of God high as the heavens. . . ." We say, for goodness' sake, not that high. It might be God's will for me to go out and work for Him. It might be His will for me to get out on a limb on some controversial issue. That is biting off a lot of trouble. Let's try something easier.

All this is not very far from any one of us, is it? One easily escapes

113

from hard things, but when we escape from them we ought to remember that we also escape from the joy of the Lord and from the
zest of being faithful workers with Him.

The last stanza of that hymn pictures a glorious possibility:

> O large and free and glorious God
> With ways exceeding kind,
> Give unto us Thy breadth of love
> In loving all mankind.

61 ❖ *Anybody's Guess*

W E WILL not read far in a daily newspaper these days without coming across the phrase that something is "anybody's guess." We read that what Russia will do about this or that is "anybody's guess." Who will win the national pennant next year is "anybody's guess," in spite of eight managers claiming that it is a certainty for their team. We see the phrase so often that many people think everything in the world is just a guess.

Some things, of course, are actually "anybody's guess." It seems to be that way with a play or a book. Even the most astute publisher or producer cannot guarantee anything. A play into which someone put nearly $100,000 this last year was taken off the stage after two performances in New York City. The producer simply guessed wrong. But there are some things in the moral and spiritual world that are not, in reality, a guess at all.

There are things which are not "anybody's guess" but somebody's faith. It was true of Columbus. The onlookers thought that it was "anybody's guess" whether there was anything out there or not. Columbus was not guessing. He had a sustaining faith. He had the evidence for that faith, enough to bank on and risk the venture. Onlookers in Philippi, when they saw the Apostle Paul land from a little ship, the first Christian missionary to Europe, might have said, "Well, it is anybody's guess whether the babbler gets anywhere." It was not a guess with Paul. It was a faith, and a faith which became great history.

There are many things which are not "anybody's guess" but somebody's experience. They have demonstrated that "it works." With the words, for instance, "My peace I give unto you," it is not a "guess" whether it works or not. It is the actual experience of multitudes of people who in times of turmoil have had the deep peace that faith in God brings. Get out of the world of guessing into the world of faith and experience.

62 ❖ *The Baby Grew Up*

THE CHRISTMAS story is the story of a baby. That is a part of its inexhaustible pull on the mind and heart of humanity. But it is also a liability. For a great many people become so entranced with the beautiful story of a baby in a manger that they miss the chief point of the story, and hence do not feel the compulsion which it lays on life. We can become so charmed with the story of a baby that we grow sentimental about it; it does not ask that we do anything about it; it does not demand any vital change in our way of thinking and living.

But the chief point of the story is that *the baby grew up!* He grew up to become the sternest challenge to a world of hard power that had ever been made. He was no sentimentalist; he was a terrible realist! Everything opposed to love and brotherhood in our world, he declared flatly, is doomed and damned—for the reason that at the center of the universe is a God of loving purpose to all men.

The great question for us is this: Is our Christmas still only a story about a baby, or is it more, a deathless story about a Man, the Son of Man, into whom the baby grew, who can redeem the world from its sins, and who calls us into partnership with his great and mighty purposes?

63 ✿ "You Can't Prove It By Me"

S OME TIME ago I was out for a Sunday afternoon drive in the company of a man distinguished in public affairs. As time went by our conversation ranged over many topics. But whether we discussed economic affairs, political matters, the weather, the price of fish, or football one refrain kept repeating itself in his speaking: "You can't prove it by me."

There seemed to be no ultimate question in any realm that could be proved by him. After we got home I wondered if there could be anything in life which he *could* prove.

From that experience it is easy to transfer our thought to the matter of the Christian faith. There are many whose lives say of the Christian faith, in effect: "You can't prove it by me." Nothing they ever do or say affords any contribution that the Christian faith is true, or that it matters one way or the other. Is that the effect Christianity has upon you? Is your only comment: "You can't prove it by me?"

There are some things about the Christian faith that we ought to be able to prove by you.

Is there anything in your manner of living that would give evidence to a bystander that life has a meaning greater than "getting and spending, laying waste our powers"? There ought to be. That is something that ought to be proved by you. Another person, looking at your life, should be able to see that you have found something which has taken you out of the prison house of yourself, given to your life a new dimension. In short, because you are a Christian you are trying to live worthy of a higher calling than any to which the ordinary life is subject.

Or, in like manner, could anyone tell from observing your life that you are in possession of a power to handle the adversities of life triumphantly? They should see it. St. Paul put it thus: "I am

117

able for all things through him who strengthens me." There you have the secret of the Christian life. You *can* prove that by living, even as Paul pleaded in another place: "Be ye transformed . . . *that ye may prove.*"

There are many things about the Christian faith that we ought to be able to prove by the Church.

For example, could we by our church, prove that ours is a God who cares supremely for all people regardless of class, race, or other barrier? Jesus said: "Go ye into *all* the world." There are some churches whose only rejoinder to that has been: "You can't prove it by us!"

The supreme act of Jesus' life—the cross—said convincingly, "You *can* prove it by me!"

By his death and resurrection all men can be convinced of the central meaning of our Christian faith, that God was in Christ reconciling the world to himself. Jesus proved that God is with us by his life, and because he proved it, we can prove it after him.

64 ❖ Incentives for Living

A SHORT TIME ago *The New York Times* published a very interesting and sad news dispatch from Lincoln, England. It was the sort of story that reappears every year or so, the story of a suicide.

A young woman, a stenographer, climbed out on the three-inch stone ledge of the central tower of the cathedral at Lincoln, England, and while a crowd 240 feet below watched silently, many of them kneeling in prayer, she jumped to her death. For an hour she stood in that perilous position, while Canon Theodore Milford of the cathedral and four members of his staff and three policemen pleaded and argued with her not to take her life, but to climb back to safety.

Now, in addition to the tragedy, there is in this scene a very pertinent question which each of us might well consider. Suppose that you were out on the ledge of the cathedral with that distracted girl, and were trying to persuade her to go on living, what would you have said?

What are to you the supreme incentives to living? It is a big question to which all Christians ought to have an answer. For that, in essence, is what the Church with its Gospel is trying to do, to persuade people to live bravely, effectively. What are the most powerful arguments?

Of course, probably no one could have done anything to prevent the suicide. There was evidently severe mental derangement. But it does pose a vital question.

Among the great incentives to living which we find in the Gospel of Christ is certainly this: You are a child of God.

Life has meaning in that relationship to God which it acquires in no other way. That has been the great incentive to multitudes. Here are the words of William James, the great philosopher, describing a time when he was in the grip of deep despair. He writes: "Fear was

119

so invasive and powerful that if I had not clung to scripture texts like 'the eternal God is my refuge,' etc., and 'Come unto me all ye that labor and are heavy laden,' etc., and 'I am the resurrection and the life,' I think I should have grown really insane."

Another incentive, and a powerful one, is the remembrance of the service one may render to others. That has kept many people going along a hard way, the realization that they counted in other lives.

There is also the incentive that "the game is not over." This day may be black. But God is still God, and tomorrow will bring a new situation if we are faithful.

65 ✿ *Your View of the World*

THERE IS no more important question for any one of us than this: "What is your view of the world?"

Here are a few varieties of world views, any one of which we may adopt.

A duck's eye view of the world. Here is the way in which the work of a notable artist for children's books, Robert McCloskey, is described:

> Preparing for his popular *Make Way for Ducklings*, he lived for some weeks with a group of mallard ducks in a studio in New York, watching and sketching them. Then, since the story involved a tour of Boston by his feathered friends, he did a good deal of crawling around Boston Common on his hands and knees to get a duck's eye view of Boston.

There is the phrase: "a duck's eye view." What would a duck's eye view of the world be? Certainly it would be a view alert for bits of food, and also for someone to quack at! Food and scolding! And we may slide into having the same kind of a view. Many people do have just this view. They are on the outlook for bits of gain, and they are alert to make a fuss at other people, just like a duck going through life! They often sound like Donald Duck.

A cat's eye view of the world. Lots of people have a cat's eye view of God's great creation. The model is in the old Mother Goose rhyme:

> Pussy cat, pussy cat, where have you been?
> I've been to London to visit the Queen.
> Pussy cat, pussy cat, what did you there?
> I frightened a little mouse under a chair.

There you have it! Confronted with all the wonders of a city and a visit to the Queen, the cat thought only of chasing some small prey, a little mouse! Lots of people do the same thing. Confronted by all the wonders and opportunities of life in this marvelous world, they see only some prey that they can pounce on, some personal advantage they can seize for themselves. Nothing else counts.

A worm's eye view of the world. A visitor to New York was asked when he returned to his home town in the Middle West: "How did you like New York?" He answered: "Well you see I spent all my time in the subway, so I got only a worm's eye view of it." Exactly! People get only a "worm's eye view" of the world when they burrow down into something just as an earthworm digs down into the ground. A person can dig down so deep into his job that it becomes his only concern, so deep into his own little house and lot that it becomes the whole earth, so deep into his own preoccupation with pleasure that he has only the view of the world that a worm gets.

A God's eye view of the world. We may have this view. And what would a God's eye view of the world be? We have one clear answer to that question. God's view of the world is from a hilltop—Calvary. The cross is the revelation of how God looks at the world in infinite love for all men, in sacrifice for their needs. When we have that view, we really *see* the world!

66 ✿ Running Away from Life

EVERY FEW weeks the newspapers carry a story of someone who has been a recluse or a hermit, who has just withdrawn from life. The story usually comes out when the body of the person is discovered. There is usually a large sum of money in the shabby quarters where the recluse died. An author, Helen Warden Erskine, has made a book out of these amazing stories and has appropriately entitled it *Out of This World*. The stories make sad and strange reading. The author tries hard to find reasons for such conduct. These people, men and women alike, were "holed" up while the rest of the world went by. She writes: "The moment I see drawn blinds, barred doors, rubble-littered areaways, holes where door bells should be, I know a hermit is apt to prowl within."

One of the most notable true stories concerned the Collyer brothers, Langley and Homer, one a former concert pianist, the other a Columbia Phi Beta Kappa. They became hermits in the late 1930's, and lived like penniless barbarians although thousands of dollars were in the room. Besieged by policemen, process servers, sheriffs, and tax people, they were "page one" hermits in the 1940's. Next to them in notoriety was a Fifth Avenue recluse, Miss Ella Wendall, who held the fort in solitary life in her home at Fifth Avenue and 39th Street while possessed of a fortune of fifty million dollars.

These stories are a reminder that there are many other people who run away from life and its duties and opportunities. Their withdrawal is not as dramatic as that of the hermits who starve in the midst of their own wealth, but it is a real withdrawal just the same. These people do not "take the veil," as they say of a woman who goes into a convent. But they have shut themselves off from the world of need and the call for expenditure of themselves in service. They have made their little self-centered universe, and in it they live and have their being. They are monarchs of all they survey, but the surveying is hardly worth the trouble because the outer fringes of the whole system is only a few feet away from their own concern. They do not live in God's world with its colorful pageant of many races, its thrilling plot, and its tense battle against evil. They have retired from the world.

It is hard to get such people to do anything that calls for personal effort. They will not take a Sunday school class. They say, airily, that they do not like to be "tied down to things," but they forget that, as Christians, we are disciples of One who was willing to be *nailed* down to a cross. They shut themselves out from the great experiences of personal growth through activity in service, and the zest of being part of "the community of the sent."

67 ✿ The Devil's Creed

SOMEONE HAS proposed an interesting question: "If the devil has a creed, what would it be?" We know the Christian Creed. What would be the creed of the forces of evil?

This question could lead to endless guessing and conjecture. We can get a clue to an answer, however, by asking: "What are the popular ideas and assertions which cause the most damage in the world?" A few of them are set out below. The point to be stressed is that these slogans or beliefs, which do cause such damage to the cause of Christianity, are the very things that easily become our own creed or belief. The reason for this is that they are easy; they follow the line of least resistance; they offer us a fine-sounding excuse for doing nothing. Hence they are a devil's creed.

The time is not ripe. This is the argument by which any good cause can be knocked on the head, because it is always true. The ideal time for any spiritual undertaking, any advance in human welfare, is never at hand. No fully ripe time ever comes. As a wise man has said, "If we wait till the time is ripe, it may be rotten." The result of saying, over and over again, "The time is not ripe," is to do nothing, ever. Was the time ripe for the beginning of Christianity in Greece and Rome? Was the time ripe for the beginning of the Evangelical Revival in eighteenth-century England? Or for the beginning of the modern missionary movement in the early nineteenth century? From the human standpoint there was no chance for any of these movements. But God had other ideas.

One person does not count. This is one of Satan's master lies. It is effective, if we do not look closely at it, for it seems to be true. It generates the feeling: "What's the use?" But history shows that this is a lie. One person does count and counts enormously.

Don't be sentimental. It is amazing how many people are scared

125

out of their real wits by this ancient scarecrow of a statement. It simply means that anything that is not hardboiled selfishness is given the false label, "sentimentalism."

The devil is called the "Father of Lies" for a very good reason!

68 ✿ The Stubs of an Old Checkbook

IN AN address on the art of biography Philip Guedalla, an eminent practitioner of the art, said that the hardest problem a biographer has is to discover just what his subject really was as a person. It is comparatively easy, he said, to find out what he *did*, and what he *said*, and where he *went*. But what kind of man he really was is a different matter. Mr. Guedalla gave as an instance his own problem in writing his biography of the Duke of Wellington. "What," he asked himself, "would be trustworthy evidence of the kind of man Wellington actually was?" He says that he found such unimpeachable evidence when he came across the stubs of Wellington's old checkbooks.

He was right, wasn't he? What could be more trustworthy evidence about us than the stubs of our old checkbooks? For there is evidence of what we really care for. The question is, how would we like to look over the stubs of our checkbooks? What sort of person would they show us to be? Then, what really ought the stubs of our checkbook show if it is to be said: "This is the checkbook of a Christian"?

69 ✿ "The Airy Grace of a Country Club"

I N AN appreciative magazine article about Frank Lloyd Wright, the architect, there was a disturbing phrase.

The article said that Mr. Wright had recently designed a church in a Western city "which had all the airy grace of a country club." What a tribute to a *church*, that it had the "airy grace of a country club"!

Of course the phrase referred merely to the architecture of the building. But, even so, should not a building erected to the worship of God suggest something more and other than the paradise of a tired businessman, with full equipment of a shady porch, luxuriant chairs, and a golf course?

The real disturbance, however, comes when we recall how easy it is for the organization itself—what ought to be, at least, the spiritual fellowship—to take on "the airy grace of a country club." A church can go in so heavily for comfort that it can lose almost unconsciously, its aspiration toward God, and its unsatisfied yearning for the salvation of the world.

Two frequent marks of a country club are its exclusiveness and its ministering to pleasure. And both of them can displace, in the life and mind of a church, its ancient passion for the souls of men. It can, and often does, grow satisfied with the exclusive fences which shut in "the best people" and shut out the rest of God's children. It can put its major emphasis on a good time, with nothing disturbing in its message or worship, nothing which causes the people to cry, "God, be merciful to me, a sinner," or any burden of duty which makes them say, "Here am I, send me."

Karl Barth has said profoundly: "Where there is no anguish in the heart, there will be no great music on the lips." Perhaps that is one reason why there has been no great compelling music on the lips of many churches.

Here is a question for us: Just how should our church differ from a country club? The answer is in the last chapter of many of Paul's epistles, in which he gives a picture of the people who made up the little church of the first century. He calls them "brothers," indicating fellowship, not for the sake of good fellowship in itself, but fellowship around a Person, and in his purpose. He calls them "workers," indicating the zealous expenditure of strength and soul. He calls them "sufferers," indicating sacrifice, withholding nothing. There was no "country club" atmosphere there.

What is our church—Club House or Power House?

70 ✿ Natural History of Nonsense

A BOOK OF fascinating interest is *The Natural History of Nonsense* by Bergen Evans. In it the author takes many of our most widely held superstitions for a merry ride. He sets about to demolish popular superstitions.

The roll call of ancient and modern superstitions is a memorable one. There is the old belief that if the world were round the people at the North and South Poles would fall off. There is the newer superstition that drunken men walk east because of the rotation of the earth; and the favorites of our childhood, that toads cause warts, that a potato in the pocket will keep away rheumatism, that a red rag is more liable to make a bull enraged than a rag of any other color.

It makes entertaining reading. But it also suggests other kinds of nonsense in the moral and spiritual world—things which are endlessly repeated and get themselves believed, but which are arrant nonsense of a particularly vicious kind.

Each of us will think of his own list, the lies in the world of religion which are truly nonsense.

Here are a few:

The feeling, so often expressed with the air of having made a fresh contribution to the world's wisdom, that "it doesn't make any difference what a person believes, it's what he *does* that counts." That makes just as much sense as to say that "it doesn't make any difference what a farmer plants, it's what he harvests that counts." In the moral and spiritual, as in agricultural life, it is what is planted that determines the harvest.

The idea, very often expressed, that "we can have a transformed world without having transformed people." True, we cannot wait for a world of saints in order to make social progress. But it is also true that we can never have a significant social whole made up of insignificant social units. No number of zeros will ever add up to any sum other than zero.

"It will all be the same in a hundred years." How many times have you heard this Prize Lie? It says, lazily, that conduct makes no difference whatever, whether one is pure or licentious, whether one is generous or stingy. It makes a tremendous difference in the eternal destiny of the soul. It makes a tremendous difference in the world.

71 ❖ Bang and Whimper

THOSE ARE tremendous words with which T. S. Eliot closes his poem, "The Hollow Men," a poem which deals among other things with men in whom religion has become an empty and impotent tradition instead of a power. He writes that the world ends, "not with a bang, but with a whimper."

In his book written just before the outbreak of World War II, Professor Frederick Schuman uses these words as a motto, as in his view depicting the "Hollow Men" in France and England and elsewhere who were not intent on saving democracy and freedom, but on appeasing Hitler in a blind defense of their money bags. Their world ended, "not with a bang, but with a whimper."

However that may be, it is easy to see the danger of having life degenerate into a whimper. A person's life may begin with a bang, that is, its early years may show an energetic approach to a task, and achievement with high purposes and unselfish aims. Then those purposes may be pared down, the unselfish vision become dimmed, thoughts of self-interest grow—and a whimper is the final chapter.

Self-pity induces a whimper; so do envy, greed, and the desire for the limelight. That is what happened to Paul's friend and follower, Demas. He began with a bang. He ended with a whimper, St. Paul wrote: "Demas hath forsaken us having loved this present world."

So it may be with a church. Its devotion to the cause of Christ may be submerged with a whimper about how tough the going is, how it cannot afford to give much to benevolences, how it is in a terribly hard field where it is not reasonable to expect much in the way of results. How well we know the sorry story, when a church becomes more interested in excuses than it is in taking up a cross and finding its life by losing it in service.

72 ✤ *"The Victim Suffered Consciousness"*

HERE IS the headline which appeared in the Poughkeepsie, New York, *Star and Enterprise,* describing an automobile accident:

TWO PERSONS HURT IN ROUTE 9-D CRASH
PEEKSKILL WOMAN SUFFERS CONSCIOUSNESS

It must be quite an accident, when a victim suffers "consciousness"! We may smile at the mistake or misprint, but, quite seriously, is there not a tremendous need for that kind of accident, in which people suffer consciousness—in which they become acutely conscious of the sufferings of others, and of the evils in the world?

It is easy to restrict ourselves to a small circle, to wall ourselves about with our own concerns, till we have no awareness of the world's ills. That was the matter with the people in Jesus' parable of the last Judgment who asked with consternation: "When saw we thee an hungered, or sick, or in prison?" It had all been going on, but they had had no consciousness of their environment. They had lived behind a protecting screen of self.

A commencement speaker once said a thing of great meaning, when he said that of all the "isms" in the world today, fascism, communism, and others, the worst is "somnambulism." True! It is going around in our sleep, not knowing or caring about what is going on in our immediate or larger world.

There is great need for a dedicated imagination. There is need for the Christlike power of putting ourselves in the place of others. We sing Frances Ridley Havergal's hymn, "Take My Life." The first lines of each of the three stanzas are, "Take my life, and let it be," "Take my voice, and let me sing," "Take my will, and make it Thine." We should add another stanza, "Take my imagination and let it be an instrument in Thy service, enabling me to see people as Jesus saw them, and move to help them as he moved."

We may ask, "Have I suffered consciousness in the deeply Christian sense? Also, How may I keep my imagination alive and reponsive?"

We can do it by keeping our eyes open. We can do it by reading. We can do it by prayer. We can do it by stopping the noisy clamor of self long enough to hear the still sad music of humanity, right at our door, and also across the seas.

73 ❊ *Anonymous*

TURN, SOMETIME, to the index of your hymn book and discover how many of the hymns were written by that great poet, Anonymous. It is a rather stirring exploration.

Every hymnbook will list at least twenty-five or thirty hymns to the credit of this unknown figure. Some of them, surprisingly enough, are the great hymns of the Church. "Come Thou Almighty King" was written by Anonymous. So was "Adeste Fideles," both words and music. So were "Fairest Lord Jesus" and "Jesus the Very Thought of Thee," and the great Easter hymn, "The Strife Is O'er, the Victory Won."

Think of launching into eternal remembrance such great hymns as those which have just been named, among the many! What a debt the Church and the world owe to the writer whose name has been forgotten!

If we start out on this line of thought and let our imagination run freely, we will have an exciting journey. How many of the great gifts to life have come from the hands of Anonymous! Who invented the wheel? Who first made use of fire? Who first pried loose a great stone with a lever? Nobody knows. His name was Anonymous.

Consider the New Testament. How many of those who served greatly the cause of Christ were without name!

There was the man, for instance, who made possible the Last Supper by allowing it to be held in his house. We do not know his name, but he was a vital part of all it has meant to the world.

There was the town clerk in Ephesus who saved the life of Paul by a flash of inspired common sense amidst hysteria. We know his position but not his name.

Two things emerge for our remembrance. One is that no one can set a limit to the amount of good a person can do if he does not care who gets the credit. The second is that if our world is ever to be truly saved, to be made secure and livable, it will be done by Anonymous.

That is, it will be done by those who do not leave their names on the great rolls of history, but who are part of the forces making for public opinion that will ultimately make a better world. That means you and me—Anonymous.

74 ❖ *What God Hath Put Asunder*

EVERYONE IS familiar with the solemn words of the marriage ceremony: "What God hath joined together, let not man put asunder."

That, of course, reaches out into many more things than the marriage ceremony. For instance, God has joined together sex and love. Let not man put them asunder. God has joined together work and happiness. When we try to separate them, we run into great trouble.

These words, however, are also true in reverse. We can say truly: "What God hath put asunder, let not man join together." A great deal of the evil in the world has come from man's effort to join together things that God has separated.

Jesus said: "You cannot serve God and Mammon." *He has put asunder the service of money as an end in itself, and the service of God.*

Many doubt that. They say: "Is that so? Just watch me! I can have the best of both worlds. I can serve God and also serve Mammon." That leads to ruin, both in personal life and in the life of society.

God has put asunder the worship of idols and the worship of God. "Thou shalt have no other gods before Me."

Yet all through history men have tried to combine the worship of some other god with the worship of God Almighty. They have made an idol out of the state holy and sacred, and they have set it up on a level with—or above—the worship of the God revealed in the Bible. We cannot join together the things which God has separated.

God has put asunder the license of immoral indulgence and the durable satisfactions of life.

Men have tried to put these two things together. They have said: "We will find the highest good in life in undisciplined appetites with no reservations." They have said: "Let us eat, drink, and be merry."

137

The end of that is a sorry type of merriment. Men have never found lasting happiness at the end of the way of indulgence. God has separated these things.

75 ❖ *"Casually Yours"*

A DEPARTMENT store advertised a new coat for college girls. It was an informal sort of affair and the advertising revealed that the store was very proud of the name of the coat. The name was "Casually Yours."

Perhaps it fits the young ladies of today. A man who is no longer young recently said he could remember that when he was in college, back in the "Stone Age," there were quite a number of girls who were *very* casually his! The advertisement goes on to boast: "This coat captures beautifully that "fine air of informal unconcern." Is not that chiefly what is the matter with the world? There is too much "fine air of informal unconcern."

The church which says to its Master, "Casually Yours," will be no agent of redemption. People who say to the rest of the world, hungry, cold, and desolate, "Casually Yours," will be no saving force for the building of a safe tomorrow or the relieving of need today. We must say to the cause of world survival and to democracy as an instrument of survival, not "Casually Yours," but "Tremendously Yours."

Clearly, too, we must say to the cause of Christ, "Tremendously Yours."

76 ❖ *Saved by an Idea*

THERE IS a striking narrative in de Harsanyi's novel of the life of Galileo, entitled *The Star Gazer*, which holds an arresting suggestion.

Young Galileo became so depressed and discouraged in his early life that he decided to drown himself. Nothing had worked out for him as he had hoped, and there seemed to be nothing to live for. He went down to the banks of the Tiber river, and paused a moment before throwing himself in. He got to thinking of his lifeless body floating in the river. But from that morbid thought his quick mind went on to raise the question, would the body float, and if so, why? Then the next step was to think of the law of specific gravity, and how it could be measured. The idea took such possession of his mind that suicide was forgotten, and he rushed home to begin the experiments which resulted in the invention of the hydrostatic scales. *He was saved by an idea!* The negative thinking which was dragging him down to death was replaced by a stronger positive thought of the measurement of specific gravity, and that truth set him free from despair.

It is a very suggestive picture of the way in which the ideas of Christianity have a saving power. Galileo stopped thinking about himself, and was saved by his mind's entering a larger realm than his own depression.

Jesus put that truth in words: "He that loseth his life shall find it."

Here are some saving ideas of the Christian gospel: the reality of a God of love, the power that comes into life when Christ is given an entrance, the forgetting of self in serving the needs of others.

77 ✿ Antiquated Geography

A GOOD question for individuals as well as for congregations is: "Is Your Map Up to Date?" How would we fare if we started out on a journey through our country with a map of the New World drawn by Capt. John Smith in 1611?

Antiquated maps have been the cause of many great calamities. The phrase is used by the historian, G. M. Trevelyan, in his book, *Social History of England*, Volume III, which deals with the eighteenth century. He writes the following about the Christian religion at that time: "The Church had antiquated maps." He points out that there was no recognition made by Church authorities of the large new suburbs of London or the growing industrial cities of Manchester, Birmingham, and others. No new parishes had been arranged to meet the spiritual needs of these multitudes of people. The same parishes which had been sufficient in the days of Queen Elizabeth were all that had been provided.

In personal life, also, our geography may be badly antiquated. Our horizons of thought and interest can be too pitifully near. Thus, there are many people in New York to whom Tenth Avenue is the Far West; Staten Island, the Deep South; and the Bronx, the North Pole. In like manner, people in Los Angeles are likely to think of Long Beach as the edge of the Orient and of Needles, Arizona, as the Far East where the sun rises.

The truth is that there is no east which is *far*. When President Eisenhower made his trip to Korea in December, 1952, he left New York at 6 A.M., arrived at San Francisco at 3 A.M. the same night, and arrived at Hawaii a little before midnight the *previous* night! That is the kind of world we live in. We have all seen drawings of old maps, which were used before the discovery of Americans, on which a river that ran around the surface of the earth is shown, and Gibraltar is the "jumping off place."

141

In our own land, churches must be alert to provide for the religious needs of new centers of population which do not show up on maps of even five years ago.

Christianity was born with a map of the known world in its hand. Its charter was: "Go ye into all the world." St. Paul had an acute sense of the map. He wrote: "Whensoever I go to Spain . . . " and "I must see Rome." Keep your map up to date!

78 ❖ A "Vulnerable Heart"

THE PHRASE above, a beautiful one, was used by a critic in describing the poet, Edna St. Vincent Millay, as revealed in the book of her letters published in the fall of 1952. He meant by it that she had a sensitive and intense capacity for feeling. He wrote: "Her devotion to her mother and sisters was far finer than most family relationships. Her friendships were as emotional as love affairs." To a friend she wrote: "Never say to me again: 'Anyway, you can make a trial of being friends with me.' I can't do things that way. I am not a tentative person."

Do we have a "vulnerable heart"? Or has it grown a hard case around it so that it is not easily touched with another's trouble or pain? Much of the agony of the world has come from the lack of vulnerable hearts in many people. Probably there was never such a demonstration of well-cased hearts as during the early nineteenth century in England when the employment of small children, often not much more than babies, in mine and factory was really a form of child murder. This happened in a so-called Christian country. Children five and six years old were employed from thirteen to sixteen hours a day. In the 1840's a large portion of the whole number of persons employed in "trades and manufactures" was under thirteen years of age. Yet when the bill to restrict the working hours of children to ten a day was up in Parliament, it was roundly defeated. It took twenty-five years of legislation to restrict a child of nine years to a sixty-nine-hour week, and that only in cotton mills! That was about twelve hours a day for six days a week, and that reduction was regarded by many as a humane achievement! No wonder Elizabeth Barrett Browning cried out:

> Do you hear the children weeping, O my brothers . . .
> They are weeping in the playtime of the others
> In the country of the free.

143

A jeweler put in his window, as an advertisement, a watch ticking in a cake of ice! Is that a picture of our hearts, ticking under the protection of cold ice, or are our hearts, like that of our Master, "vulnerable"?

79 ✿ "Jesus Himself Drew Near"

THERE IS a sentence in the story of the walk to Emmaus in the gospel of Luke which is a wonderful text and which fits closely the life of an individual, of a church, and of the world. Here it is: "And it came to pass, while they communed and questioned together, Jesus himself drew near."

We spend our lives talking and communing and discussing together. It is not empty chatter, but our reasonable service. That is the way we learn, the way teaching is done. Jesus himself spent much of his life communing and questioning with people.

It is our great hope that as people discuss and talk *Jesus himself draws near*.

That is true in individual lives. There is so much in religion that calls for discussion. Men and women have been busy with it and rightly. Questions such as "What is the meaning of our faith?" and "What is the right thing to do?" call for communing and reasoning. Into the midst of this, Jesus himself has drawn near and lifted the whole matter of religious faith out of the realm of the academic into the realm of experience, out of secondhand opinion into that of the living Christ in life.

This is true of a congregation as well. There is much necessary discussion on ways and means. We need not less of it, but more of it. We should bring to the work of the church the clearest thinking and the most practical wisdom that we can attain. But there is always the danger of the goal being lost in discussion of the means. But there is the great hope of the miracle of Emmaus, that Jesus himself will draw near, fill the church with his spirit and his own life, so that the church becomes truly what it may be, the body of Christ.

Think of the endless discussion that goes on in the world over social and economic and international questions. What is the best way to insure human survival? How may the evils of aggressive nationalism

145

be curbed or cured? There will be no real solution until Jesus himself draws near the council tables and the legislatures, and his goals and his spirit be recognized and followed, so that the New Testament vision of one family in God may be realized.

80 ❖ *Are You a Fanatic?*

ONE OF the interesting books of recent years is *Windows for the Crown Prince*, by Elizabeth Gray Vining. Mrs. Vining is the woman selected as a tutor to the Crown Prince of Japan. She spent two highly successful years in that important post and the book is the record of her experiences.

In the book there is the story of the request of the Emperor of Japan for the assignment of a tutor. Members of the court asked Dr. Stoddard, President of the University of Illinois, to find an American, "a Christian but not a fanatic," and someone new to Japan.

The phrase which calls for attention here is the one, "*not a fanatic.*" Two things stand out. One is that agreement should be given for the preference for a Christian who is not a "fanatic." In that sense, the word "fanatic" represents a thoroughly bad type of person. A fanatic may be a Christian who stands for impertinent things, that is, things which are not pertinent to the essential Christian faith. A fanatic is often concerned for the shibboleths of a political party, or for the details of a legalistic code. There have been fanatics who declared that a person who cooked food on Sunday could not be a Christian. Fanatics in Scotland for years would not eat potatoes because they are not mentioned in the Bible. The true Christian is not a fanatic in this sense. The New Testament gives us the true test of a Christian: "As many as are led by the Spirit of God, they are the sons of God."

But, we should watch out for another use of the term "fanatic," an unfair use, but a very common one. For too many people outside of the Church and completely outside of Christian allegiance a "fanatic" means anyone who takes his religion seriously. Thus, a person who believes firmly that "God was in Christ reconciling the world to Himself" is called a narrow, dogmatic "fanatic." To them Christianity is just moralistic teaching. They miss nothing in Christianity except the main point, that it is a gospel of redemption in Christ.

147

So the same is true concerning Christian conduct. There are hosts of people who regard anyone who does not use alcoholic liquor as a fanatic. So also, others try diligently to spread the idea that persons who bring Christian teaching into relation to the world, to labor conditions, or to war are meddling fanatics. This same type of person started the hue and cry against St. Paul when he contended for the rights of God's children.

Go over Christian history and you will see that the great servants of God and man through the gospel were "fanatics" in the sense that they had an unshakable conviction that Jesus Christ is Lord of all life. In this high sense, God grant that we may all be what is called a "fanatic"!

81 ❋ The Grumbler

A VERY thoughtful English preacher, a Roman Catholic priest, Ronald Knox, has published a book of arresting sermons based on Biblical passages. One of them is entitled "Careful and Troubled." It is concerned with the familiar story of Mary and Martha in the home in Bethany when Jesus was there for dinner. The author makes the point, and it is well worth noting, that our Lord's rebuke to Martha is not so much against those who bustle, as against those who *grumble*. That was what Martha was doing when she asked Jesus to rebuke Mary for not helping get the dinner ready. She was grumbling. She thought Mary should help, "plate breaker as she probably was." We can still detect in Martha's sharp words the note of grumbling.

Now, couple with this story the words in the second chapter of Philippians, verse 14: "Do all things without grumbling." The habit of grumbling is not a minor affair, for it can spoil the whole climate of a life. To allow oneself to become a "gloomy Gus" is a major affliction, for it gets one into the state where nothing is right, something is the matter with everything. Someone said, when he heard of the death of Matthew Arnold: "Poor Matthew, he won't like God." That was certainly unfair, but it does describe the critical, often scolding attitude of Matthew Arnold. It is a dangerous attitude of mind and heart, because it shuts God completely out of life. There is no note of thanksgiving which preserves life from being "sour."

This grumbling habit also shuts out all joy in service. A person gets too occupied with his complaints to think about the needs of others. The constant clang of the riveting machine of his own dissatisfaction shuts out the still small voice of God and of human need.

82 ✿ Two Kinds of Prayer

ONE OF the passages of modern poetry that is familiar to a great many people, and ought to be familiar to many more, occurs toward the end of W. H. Auden's long poem, *A Christmas Oratorio*. The poet is picturing the low levels to which a speaker fears prayer may descend if the worship of Jesus becomes a mere cult. To stress his point, he gives a sample, full of intended anachronisms, to show what he means by the degeneracy of prayer. Here is a typical prayer which he says is the kind that may be offered:

O God, put away justice and truth, for we cannot understand them and do not want them. Eternity would bore us dreadfully. Leave Thy heavens and come down to our earth of highways and aeroplanes. Become our uncle, look after baby, escort madam to the opera, amuse grandfather. And please, God, introduce Muriel to a handsome naval officer.

Shocking? Of course! It was meant to shock. But after all, is it not uncomfortably near to many prayers that are offered in the desire to make God a sort of errand boy for our convenience?

Contrast with this the true prayer, which Jesus gave in words and lived in action. He gave it in words when he told his disciples: "After this manner, pray." That prayer asked: "Thy will be done." Jesus lived that prayer in action in the garden of Gethsemane when he said again and again: "Not my will, but thine be done."

To which of these models do our habitual prayers come nearest?

83 ❖ *Missing the Cue*

A VERY unusual occurrence marked a concert at the Royal Festival Hall in London in 1952. The conductor, Dr. Boyd Neel, came to the passage of a piece of music, "The Banks of the Green Willow," which called for solo parts by the French horns. To his embarrassment instead of the solos, there was a tremendous silence. The horn players were all backstage. They had missed their cue for the only part in which they were required!

It is easy to get engaged in things so deeply that we "miss our cue" as the horn players did; that is, we miss the call for our action. Jesus was ever on the alert for the sign for his action in behalf of people in need. He heard the cry of blind Bartimeus on the roadside at Jericho, when his disciples paid no attention to it. He could tell when a timorous woman touched the hem of his garment in faith. Jesus knew the time to set his face to go to Jerusalem.

How many times when there is a cue for us to step in helpfully do we miss it because our own clanging desires make such a din that we do not hear it. It may be the unspoken word indicating need of friendship, of counsel, of fortifying for a difficult experience. The situation called for our help, but we missed the cue. Sometimes a sign indicates that we are needed in a struggle, such as against liquor or vice in a community. There is a need for our help to be given. Fifty years ago there was a distinct cue for Christian evangelization in Japan on a large scale. The mind of Japan was open as the mind of a nation had hardly ever been. But the churches missed the cue. The response to that opportunity was inadequate. Many feel strongly that if the churches had sent a few thousand missionaries then we would not have needed to send hundreds of thousands of soldiers fifty years later. Today the great opportunity, the tremendous need is India. Will we miss the cue again?

84 ✿ *Playing for Safety*

THERE IS a true and notable sentence in the recent book, *Rumor and Reflection*, by the art critic, Bernard Berenson. In writing about aristocratic classes, he says: "A class begins to decline when it begins to play for safety, for securing its privilege, power, wealth, and, while sitting tight on its money bags, opposes innovation."

Think it over. Then let us pray that it may not happen to us. It can happen to a person. He begins to go to pieces, morally and spiritually, when he begins to play for safety. That is important to remember in a time when the desire for security has become a dominating concern. When the time comes to stand up and be counted for a good cause, the person who plays for safety will say to himself: "Don't be a fool. Pipe down. Why stick your neck out?" So his neck becomes more important than his soul. About the church he will say: "Watch out, don't get in too deep." The concern for material safety will blind a person to the fact that he does not really get into the Christian life until he gets in deep.

Playing for safety threatens a church in the same way. If a church has no great desire except to balance the budget, it is not a church of the Christ who gave his life a ransom for many. Jesus could have had security by staying away from the place of danger, Jerusalem. Paul could have had safety by giving up his preaching. The Pilgrims who came to America could have had safety by remaining in Holland. With Jesus, it was the joy that was set before him which dominated him, not safety. His purpose was to do his Father's will. So with his loyal disciples. The church that never reaches out soon passes out.

85 ✳ *Summoning the Devil*

THIS DESCRIPTION of the young Robert Louis Stevenson, found in the recent life by J. C. Furnas, *Voyage to Windward*, will bring a smile to the face of the reader. The boy Stevenson, full of curiosity and superstition, is thus described:

Even in late adolescence he frightened himself badly by meticulously carrying out a formula for summoning the devil which he had encountered in a book.

What a strange idea—summoning the devil! As though there were any form of words which could bring Satan immediately to us. But wait a minute! Is it such a strange idea, after all? Do we not really "summon the devil" to come to us in attitudes and actions which we take?

Some people will reply to that: "Nonsense! I do not believe in a personal devil with horns and hoofs." All right, leave the horns and hoofs out of it. If you are not deaf, dumb, and blind, you do believe in the reality of evil and in its power. We can and do think and act in ways that serve as an invitation for evil to come and have power over us.

One real way of summoning the devil is that expressed in the old adage: "*Satan finds work for idle hands to do.*" Old but, unfortunately, true. Nature abhors a vacuum. So does the mind. If it is empty, if our hands are unoccupied, it is a clear invitation for evil to come in.

Evil companions make an excellent summoning of evil. We tend to succumb to our environment, and, if we keep company in which "everybody's doing it," we will soon be doing it too!

Failing to be watchful against letting our guards down on conduct often results in an urgent invitation to the devil. In the Gospel of Matthew there is the injunction: "Watch and pray." If we fail to watch for the first approach of evil, we leave the doors wide open.

Ambition can become an open door to evil. When a man wants position or power or success or a fortune more than anything else, we can expect moral and spiritual compromises. The words which Shakespeare puts into the mouth of the fallen Cardinal Woolsey are always in order: "I charge thee, Cromwell, put away ambition. By that sin fell the angels."

When we allow our own inner religious life to die down, when our devotion to Christ dwindles to what has been called a "tired friendship," there is not enough inner force to resist the onslaughts of temptation to evil.

Against all these invitations to evil, there is the possibility of a summons to God through prayer, through the devotion of the heart and mind, which can be a counteracting power.

86 ✿ Hideout

THE WORD "Zoar," as the name of a place, is not a familiar one except to a few Bible students. Yet in the days of the Puritans, back in the seventeenth century, it was a very familiar name because in those days the majority of people were far, far more familiar with the Bible than are most people today. The word came to be a symbol for a safe place of escape.

The name of the town of Zoar is found in the 19th Chapter of *Genesis*, in the story of Lot's escape from the doomed and burning city of Sodom. Lot was allowed to escape to the little town of Zoar where he was safe. Thus the name was used for any "hideout." It is so used in an entry in the journal of John Evelyn of London. Thus, during the terrible days of the big fire and plague in London in the year 1666, we read this entry:

> Blessing and adoring the distinguishing mercy of God to me and mine, who in the midst of this ruin were, like Lot, in my little Zoar, safe and sound.

Could anything be more shameful? There was all the agony and suffering in stricken London, but what did Mr. Evelyn care, as long as he had a "little Zoar," a place of escape, where he and his family could be safe and sound? His words show the danger of any giving of thanks in which there appears complacency, self-satisfaction, self-righteousness, and callousness to need.

Look at the words of Mr. Evelyn. Do we have any "little Zoar" where we escape from facing need and doing anything about it? Do we have places of escape where nothing matters much except our own security and comfort? All too often we do. We can make an escape out of our *home*. Of course, home ought to be a haven of refuge. But it ought also to be a harbor, a place from which, refreshed, we go out on errands of service to the world outside the four walls of our refuge. We need to watch lest the theme song of our home becomes that miserable song: "Let the rest of the world go by." It is well said that the family that is all wrapped up in itself makes a very small package.

We can make our *community* a place of escape, a "little Zoar" where we give no thought to the larger regions of the rest of the country or the world. Like John Evelyn, we can be happy as long as we are safe, even though disaster overwhelms other places.

People have made little isles of safety out of their *church*. Like a parrot repeating: "Polly wants a cracker," they say the old words: "We have all we can do to take care of ourselves. Don't go taking up any collections for the ends of the earth." If that is the feeling of a church, it is no longer a church of Him who said: "Go ye into all the world." It has dwindled down until it becomes "The Zoar Memorial Church." When a church hides from human need, it hides from God.

87 ❖ How Not to Pray

I T IS often very effective to approach a great subject from the negative side. Jesus did it. He said: "Be not as the Pharisees who make long prayers," and then he went on to describe them in vivid terms. Many of his parables deal with the negative aspect of life: what not to do, as with the house built on sand, the man who buried his talent, the foolish girls who wasted their oil, and many others.

The negative never can take the place of the positive. But an exploration of how *not* to pray, with examples, may well clear the way for teaching *how* to pray.

Here are a few well-known samples of how not to pray. The first is from a poem by a Frenchman, Jules Romain, in which he gives the prayer of a woman:

> O God in heaven, vouchsafe to cure my leg.
> Matter burst from it yesterday. My God,
> Vouchsafe to fill my shop with customers.
> Help me to find out if my servant John
> Is robbing me. O God, cure my sore eyes!
> Save me, my God, from being drunk so often!
> Lord, let my son pass his examination!

That is not prayer. It is just futile screaming of orders to an errand boy. God is not an errand boy.

Here is a prayer by one of the most completely self-centered people who ever lived, Marie Bashkirtseff, a young Russian girl, whose *Journal* was published in 1885:

My God, grant that I may never have the small pox, and that I may remain pretty; that I may have a beautiful voice, and that I may be happily married.

That was not the kind of thing Jesus had in mind when he said: "After this manner pray ye!"

88 ❖ 'A Company on a Side Street"

A FEW YEARS ago a labor union official and a minister were campaigning together for many issues in social welfare in an eastern state. Though poles apart in their thinking on many matters, they had deep respect for each other. The trade union official had no use for the Church, and was emphatic in his opinion that it was all nonsense and had no relation to human needs.

On one occasion he declared to his preacher friend: "The Church is only a little company of people on a side street, singing ditties about heaven." The preacher was ready to admit that the force of the Church on social issues should have been stronger and more continuous. But, beyond that, he seized on the words of commendation as a real tribute. And they are.

The greatest forces in history for human advancement have been "little companies of people on a side street, singing ditties about heaven," if one wants to phrase it in that contemptuous way.

Take first-century Rome, for instance. Today, the traveler can go in a couple of hours, from the ruins of the Coliseum, where thousands gathered for spectacles of barbaric slaughter, to the relics of the catacombs, where another company gathered. There was an underground room, hardly large enough to accommodate more than twenty-five people, compared to the Coliseum, which was filled with fifty thousand. In the catacombs was a "little company," not on a side street, but buried away underground. But the little company was far more profoundly important and influential than the fifty thousand spectators at gladiatorial games. The future was with them, in the power of their gospel and fellowship.

It has always been so. In Leyden in Holland, in the second decade of the seventeenth century, there was another little company of people on a side street singing ditties about heaven. No one paid much attention to them. But that little company were the Pilgrims, many of whom emigrated to America on the *Mayflower* in 1620. "A little company," indeed!

So in England in the eighteenth century there were other little companies, singing the "ditties" of the Evangelical Revival which swept over England and created a new spiritual climate, leaving a deep and lasting mark on the world. Compared with these little groups, all the gatherings at the Royal Court were trivial affairs.

There is another little group—this church. Here we are, not on one of the main corners of the town. But in God's providence, this group may be the power of God, as others were in history, building in the city's life a highway for our God.

89 ✿ Imagine That!

NOT LONG ago a man sat in a train going from Philadelphia to Harrisburg, and listened to a conversation between two women in the seat ahead of him. He could not help overhearing it. The shrill voice of one of the women would have drowned out the Last Trumpet itself.

It is incorrect to call the talk conversation. It was a monologue by one woman. The best the other could do was to interject a quick exclamation, or a sigh, while the first was drawing a breath for new onslaught. The second woman kept saying, over and over again, "Imagine that!" a rough equivalent for "Is that so?" or "You don't say!" or "Not really!"

For quite a time after the trip was over, the man kept saying as a kind of echo: "Imagine that!" Then it occurred to him that the words did express both a great need of life and the power of imagination. Nothing is more needed for meeting in any way the ills of life, as they rest on other people, than the power to "imagine that," the power to put ourselves in their places.

Evil is not only or even chiefly the work of villains; it is allowed to go on by people without imagination. We are all familiar with the powerful expression of that truth by Bernard Shaw in the final act of *St. Joan*. De Stogumber, one of the judges who condemned Joan of Arc to the stake, after the burning says: "I did a very cruel thing once because I did not know what cruelty was like; I had not seen it, you know."

Then Bishop Cauchon gives him the withering answer: "Must then a Christ perish in torment in every age to save those who have no imagination?"

There is constant need of the consecrated use of our God-given faculty of making pictures of the lives of others, of feeling how the burdens of life rest heavily and cut cruelly on their shoulders.

160

The dedication of our power of imagination will also give us a vision of a world from which the massive evils of war and exploitation have been removed. We can then see the possibilities of our world, as the author of the Book of Revelation saw a city of God coming down out of Heaven. Where there is no such vision, the people perish.

Also, we can picture ourselves. We can "imagine that"—imagine ourselves not as we are, in uncertain and undependable loyalty, but as we may be, held in the power of God in steady discipleship. If we imagine that, it will be an upward pull on our lives.

90 ✿ A World Gone Sane

CONSIDER THIS arresting question by H. G. Wells: "What would a world of human beings gone sane be like?"

That question is asked in Wells' book, *Star Begotten,* published in 1937, just two years before the outbreak of World War II.

It is the reverse of the usual exclamation. We hear much lamenting about a world gone "insane." The war gave a complete picture of what a world gone insane would be like. In fact, the whole decade from 1939 to 1949 might truly be labeled "Life and Death in a Madhouse."

But we have not given as much attention to following out the question, What would a world gone *sane* look like? The dictionary gives two principal definitions of the word "sane." One is "free from mental derangement"; the other is "having or showing reason." Both definitions have pertinent meaning for the present and future of the world. We have suffered violent mental derangements which have led us off into paths of disastrous fantasy; and we have shown, in vital ways, little reason.

A world gone sane would put human life and welfare at the center. When something else is the chief desire of men and nations, there has followed what Hardy calls "the long drip of human tears." Nations have been deranged by the quest for power, with the world in the last ten years wasting its substance in destruction. Even now, over three-fourths of the world's income goes into paying for past and future wars. No wonder it has been suggested that the other planets must use this one as their insane asylum.

In a world gone sane, *people would seek the things which bring lasting satisfaction.* Too many millions spend their substance for "things which are not bread." They seek the temporary stimulants which gratify only a part of their nature, and bring no lasting joy. So we have the spectacle of multitudes who have everything to live *on,*

162

and nothing to live *for* or to live *by*. "Man shall not live by bread alone." A sane world would realize that ancient truth.

A world gone sane would see that *adjustment to the moral and spiritual order is the indispensable condition of human survival and welfare*. Take the illustration of a ship's compass. A compass "gone mad" is one which does not respond to the pull of the Pole. When that happens, the ship goes on the rocks or becomes a derelict. A compass gone sane is one which does keep its obedience to the North Star. And a world gone sane is one which responds to the true north of life, the law of God.

Two things emerge from this question. A sane world would be the world of Jesus—the world he lived in and described. The mind of Christ is the only truly sane mind. Also, the goal of the Church's action and life is to bring the sanity of Jesus to a mad world.

91 ❖ Growing Up to Maturity

THERE ARE many aspects of maturity. Mental and spiritual maturity mean, for one thing, that a person escapes from the nursery, from the playpen of childish desires with its insistence on "I, I, I," and the petulant scream of "Me, Me, Me." Paul urges: "In mind be men."

One true mark of maturity is to have standards of criticism for our world. Mr. Van Wyck Brooks, in his book, *The Confident Years*, gives a clear picture of this mark of growing up in his words about the American novelist, Booth Tarkington:

. . . The trouble with Tarkington was not that he loved the well-to-do Hoosiers he wrote about, but that he accepted so readily their Philistine standards. He was not sufficiently detached from his world to criticize its values, which is merely a way of saying that he never grew up . . .

Notice carefully the sentence: ". . . not sufficiently detached from his world to criticize its values." This is one mark of a mature Christian mind—to look at our world through other eyes, with other values than those of the world itself; and to look at the world through the eyes of Jesus. This idea is glimpsed in the plea of St. Paul: "Be not conformed to this world, but be ye renewed." There is a Christian detachment from the world in our thinking, so that we may criticize the things the world puts first in importance, and put in their stead Jesus' scale of most important things: "Seek ye first the kingdom of God."

Jesus himself did exactly that. He was detached from the codes of the Pharisees. He could bring criticism to the traditions which said that the tithing of mint, anise, and cummin was more important than mercy and justice. He had a higher attachment: "My meat is to do the will of him that sent me."

So it is a mark of Christian maturity to criticize the accepted values of many people and institutions in our day, the acquisitiveness, the scramble for power, the material prizes.

"When I became a man," I put away immature standards of measurement and looked at the world as Jesus looked at it, measuring its value by his mind and teaching.

92 ✿ *When You Can't Do Anything*

A MAN asked his minister a pointed question: "What do you
do when you can't do anything?" This question reflects a
very common mood. In so many ways the world seems going
to disaster. So many evil things prevail of which we do not approve.
Yet, in ourselves, we seem to be helpless to do anything. What do we
do then? Just sit at a wailing wall and weep?

There is an answer, or at least a guide to conduct, in the actions
of a crowd that once faced a hard situation in which they could do
absolutely nothing. And yet, they did much.

It was the group of disciples of Jesus who watched the crucifixion.
These are tragic words we read in the Gospels: "They stood there
watching." There was the best they had known, the hope of the future,
gone down in defeat. Yet they refused to say that wrong was right.
That is one thing we can do and it is a big thing. They did not say:
"Well, that shows that Pilate was right and Jesus was wrong." No
matter how powerful wrong seems to be, we can refuse to call it right.

Again, they held that God was more powerful than Rome. We can
hold to a faith in a moral and spiritual power in the universe. The
evidence was all against them. But we can see now that the visible
evidence was all wrong. When men hold the faith in the power and
love of God, they furnish Him a leverage in their own lives for His
saving action.

In the third place, these disciples held together and laid the foundation for the growth of the Church which proved to be a greater and
more lasting power than Rome.

93 ✿ *Find Yourself in This Picture*

DID YOU ever see a person looking at a photograph of a group of which he was a member? He searches eagerly to find his own picture. One concern dominates him: "How did I come out?" To notice this is not cynicism but realism. We are all inevitably interested in what concerns us.

Here is a similar game you may try with another picture. It may prove to be a disturbing, but a rewarding thing.

The picture is the large painting by Robert Haydon of Christ entering Jerusalem. This is how it is described in Hewlett's life of Keats, *Adonais*—

Christ's Entry in Jerusalem, now in St. Mary's Seminary, Norwood, Ohio, shows Christ riding on an ass, and closely surrounded by a throng of people. In imitation of Old Masters, Haydon put in figures of modern historical personages, and also of living persons. Voltaire, at this time the hero of the liberal free-thinkers, and the devil of the orthodox, was put in as a smiling scoffer; Sir Isaac Newton as a believer; Hazlitt as a detached observer; Wordsworth as a devout man; and Keats, a bright amazed face in the background.

Take it from there! Think of Christ in our world and his cause in the world. Then think of yourself and your actions and attitudes. How would you find yourself in that picture? What would best represent your habitual conduct? Would you be a "smiling scoffer" or a "detached observer"? Would there be any "bright amazement" in your face?

We *are* in the crowd which watches Christ coming into our world. What would be the truest painting of ourselves in that picture?

94 ✿ "Like Something Was Going to Happen"

THERE IS a striking figure of speech in a story by Ring Lardner entitled "Big Town Story." It is the comment of Mr. Big on his expensive hotel life: "Everybody puts on their evening clothes, like something was going to happen, but it don't."

Incidentally, that is worth a preacher's notice as a description of a kind of sermon, one that gets "all dressed up in evening clothes," correct with white tie and shirt, introduction and theme, so that it looks "as though something was going to happen, but it don't."

How closely the words fit many individuals' lives. "As though something were going to happen." There is often a promising beginning, the hint of great possibilities for the life; "it doth not yet appear what it shall be." Then nothing happens! It goes into dull, heavy clouds of mediocrity. What *does* hinder so many lives from reaching any moral and spiritual distinction? What are common causes of such an anticlimax? We will find much suggestion on this in the Parable of the Sower and the Soils.

The same thing all too often occurs in the life of a church. It is all dressed up "in evening clothes, as though something was going to happen." A beautiful building and fine equipment are all ready for big business, as though a saving force were to be unleashed in the community and the world. Then it goes into a dull routine. Nothing that remotely suggests the glowing words of the Book of Acts about an earlier church: "The place where they prayed was shaken."

168

95 ❖ Is Jesus a "Back Number"?

THERE IS a much-quoted remark of D. H. Lawrence, written in a letter to Katherine Mansfield. He wrote, "Cheer up, Kate, Jesus is a back number." Just what cheer that might bring to a young woman dying of tuberculosis does not appear! But let that pass.

What we cannot let pass is the assertion: "Jesus is a back number." So much in our present world contradicts it. The daily newspapers, to say nothing of books, print news that demonstrates that, in many very real ways, history is a process of overtaking the insights and teachings of Jesus.

Many people, particularly some of the scholars, scientists, and philosophers, seem to throw the gospels away and quote from memory. Bertrand Russell is a good example of this. Several years ago, looking around on the shambles that man has made out of his world, he came up with the conclusion that what was necessary was "to diminish the instincts that center around possession." A profound observation! The only trouble was that it was made nineteen hundred years before Mr. Russell discovered it. It was made by Jesus, more succinctly and deeply, when he said: "He that loseth his life shall find it." Another "discovery" that Mr. Russell reported was very remarkable. In an address at Columbia University, it was rather amusing to see and hear the apologies and hesitations with which he made his announcement that Christian love was the world's greatest need. Here it is, with all the apologies left in:

The root of the matter (if we want a stable world) is a very simple and old-fashioned thing, so simple that I am almost ashamed to mention it for fear of the derisive smile with which wise cynics will greet my words. The thing I mean is love, Christian love, or compassion. If you feel this you have a motive for existence, a reason for courage, an imperative necessity for intellectual honesty.

169

Two more recent examples of getting abreast of Jesus have appeared. Dr. William C. Menninger, the distinguished psychiatrist, said:

If we could love our neighbors as ourselves we could have Utopia. In fact, the hope of the world rests on our capacity to love, because it is the only way to neutralize the hate within us that comes from the deepest layers of our personality.

Let's see. Didn't Jesus say: "A new commandment I give unto you, that you love one another"?

Dr. Clarence P. Oberndorf, professor of psychiatry at Columbia University, told a convention of psychologists that "mental health depends upon the extent of awareness that a person has attained in his relation with his fellow beings."

That sounds familiar, doesn't it? Jesus is the "great contemporary."

96 ✿ *Going to the Dogs*

THE FOLLOWING dispatch—honest, I am not fooling!—was sent out over the Associated Press, with the date line, Denver, Col., Nov. 1952:

Pal, a 15 year old dog of indefinite breed, went to the grave yesterday with a funeral his master estimated cost $1,000.

Fred Schmitt rated Pal above all the other pets on his 40 acre farm north of Denver. And there are lots of pets—50 dogs, 75 cats, 4 horses and many pigeons.

Mourners, friends of Schmitt, and of his wife and the dog, Pal, filed by the mahogany casket to look at Pal for the last time. A minister spoke. The casket, made by Schmitt, was banked with flowers. Schmitt said: "That dog was my whole life."

That was really "going to the dogs"!

But it was no worse than many other things, not so sensational. Whenever a person says about anything material: "That was my whole life," he proclaims himself an idol worshiper; he proclaims that he lives in a world too small for a son of God. A man's pets, or his business, even his home and family are not big enough for him to say of them: "That was my whole life." Only one thing is big enough. Paul said it: "For to me to live is Christ." He had a true measure of life when he said: "I must see Rome." To make Christ the Master of life and to give ourselves to his purposes is to find the life which is life indeed.

OLIVER WENDELL HOLMES once wrote that "heredity is
like an omnibus, in which all our ancestors are packed.
Every once in a while," he wrote, "one of our ancestors puts
his head out of the window and embarrasses us." By that he meant
that some act of ours may be explained by an inherited trait from
some forgotten ancestor.

It would be an easy alibi if we could put the blame for all our fail-
ings and sins onto one of our ancestors! Nevertheless, physically,
there is much truth to Dr. Holmes' amusing picture. We do inherit
from our forefathers.

Often, also, this truth about being embarrassed by our ancestors is
seen at work when children and grandchildren are covered with shame
over the actions of their fathers or grandfathers.

The truth also works the other way, and that is our concern here.

Great and noble ancestors can be an embarrassment by the necessity they lay upon their descendants to live up to them. They lay
upon their descendants the obligation not to "let them down." That
is true in a family. There is a family tradition to be upheld, a tradition of integrity. Nothing can be a finer force in the life of a person
than the realization that he must prove worthy of his heritage.

This is deeply true of the Christian church. We have great spiritual
ancestors who are an "embarrassment" to us in that they set a high
mark for us to live up to. We are "surrounded by a great cloud of wit-
nesses." What ancestors we have in the first Christian century—men
and women who said, at the cost of their lives: "We must obey God
rather than man." Great ancestors in the company who went out to
carry the gospel to Europe; in those who later carried it across the
seas to America; in those who first carried it to the Far East. We
ought to be shamefully embarrassed if we do not, in our day, show
any of their qualities.

The same is true of denominational fathers and mothers. Congregationalists may well ask if they match their fathers, who came over to New England, in the seriousness with which they take their faith and endeavor to do what they believe to be the will of God. Methodists may well ask if they resemble at all the courageous John Wesley who said: "Always look a mob in the face," and "Fear nothing but sin." Lutherans may ask: "Is the courage of Martin Luther an embarrassment to us in our spineless timidity, or an inspiration to show his valiant heart in our own time?" Baptists may ask if Roger Williams, that dauntless fighter for liberty, would recognize them as fellow spirits. So with other noble "founding fathers."

98 ❖ "This Little Pig Went to Market"

THIS SHORT meditation is concerned with nothing more terrifying than a child's piggy bank, which is almost standard equipment for any home. The piggy bank is a teacher and entertainer for children. These words about it should not be read as though they were uttered in a solemn tone, or raising a great moral issue about an innocent device for teaching a child thrift. They are just some thoughts that occurred to one onlooker for a few months at a domestic drama with four characters: Mother, Father, Johnnie and a Piggy Bank.

Johnnie was being given a thorough training in thrift and saving. Such encouragements as these were daily occurrences: "Put your nickel into the piggy bank, sweetheart. Listen. Hear it? Ping, ping, ping." And, "Isn't it nice to hear the pennies dropping into the bank? Pretty soon there will be a hundred of them!" So Johnnie is getting conditioned to like the ping of a coin dropped into the china bank more than the passing delight of an ice cream cone at the corner drugstore.

So, the piggy bank may help the young financier to grow up into a Pig. Why not? All the time the boy hears: "Piggy, piggy, piggy." And the ping, ping, ping of savings may be the sweetest music he knows. The epitaph on such a concentrated course of training in thrift may be: "This little pig went to market."

All this adds up to one point, a big one, though it may seem to have a trivial connection here. How much more detailed, continuous, and emphatic is the usual training parents give their children in thrift, than is the training they give in generosity. Think it over. That training in giving is so often incidental, accidental, and occasional. It may be nothing more than giving the child a nickel or a dime to take to

Sunday School. There is little or nothing done to condition the child to the pleasure of actually giving something that is his own and that he gives of his own free will because he wants to do it. But generosity is at the very center of Christian character. Is there not a great and ever-present need to provide for our children training and experience in giving, far more than in saving? If we do not do this, how can we expect to have children grow up into sympathetic, sensitive, generous Christian personalities?

99 ❖ *How Irritable Are You?*

T HE WORD "irritable" usually has a bad meaning for us. If we are told that a man is a very irritable person, our tendency is to give him a wide berth. We do not like violent explosions such as used to be pictured in the comic cartoon of "'The Terrible Tempered Mr. Bang" of several years ago. Our feeling is right. For in that sense, an irritable man is frequently an overgrown baby who has never grown up. He grows purple in the face and begins to scream when anyone touches his rattle.

But in the biological world, the word is used in a very different and primary sense. There it means the capacity of an organism to respond to outside stimuli. It is rightly made the measure of the ascent in the scale of life. The more sensitive the capacity to respond, the higher up the creature is in the scale of life. The clam is low down on the scale, because its nervous organization does not allow much of a response. You never heard of a clam with a nervous breakdown. There is nothing to break down. But when you get up in the biological scale and come to man, there is a delicate and sensitive nervous system that gives man great powers, and also, the capacity for pain.

The same mark applies to the life of the soul. Have we the capacity to respond to the stimulus of need around us? If we have, we share in the "life which is life indeed." If we have not, we are still outside of our highest heritage as humans. Then, in the spiritual scale we are "low grade animals," like the clam in the physical scale.

Recall how irritable, in that high sense, Jesus was. He had an exquisite response to need whenever he met it. Others around him did not see it, but he did. A blind man sat by the roadside and cried in desperation: "Jesus, thou Son of David, have mercy on me!" The bystanders had no response to that need. They were not "irritable" to the stimulus of suffering. All they could do was to shout at the blind man, "Oh, shut up." Jesus said: "Come here." Which is most like our usual response to need?

Unless we make habitual responses our nerves of sympathy deaden, and we go downward in the scale of life. Paralysis sets in so easily, awareness of need becomes dull, and as far as the human family is concerned, a well-dressed corpse is walking down the street, a case of walking paralysis.

100 ✣ "I Want To Be a Christian— in My Head"

WHO HAS not heard the familiar Negro spiritual sung with great effect: "Lord, I want to be a Christian in my heart"?

The haunting music and the deep sincerity give it a stirring and moving quality. And it is profoundly true. To be a genuine Christian one must be a Christian in the *heart*; that is, to have an experience that is felt, and not something that has been merely heard, or read about, or memorized out of a book.

Yet it is not enough to be a Christian *in the heart*. There has often been a fatal and false separation between heart and mind. We must be Christians in our *minds*. If we leave out the mind, we leave out what Jesus called the first great commandment, which included the command: "Thou shalt love thy God with all thy mind." St. Paul echoes it: "In mind be men."

Part of the world's trouble has been too much Christianity of the heart, but not of the head. What God hath joined together, let not man put asunder. God has joined together heart and head, so that the whole being is to be dedicated to God. Someone said of an earnest but bumbling Christian: "He has a heart of gold and a head full of feathers." Feathers in the head are not good enough for God's service!

So much of what passes, wrongly, for religion of the heart, is merely sentimentalism. Here are two of the best definitions of sentimentality: "A sentimentalist is one who considers ends without means." Also, "A sentimentalist is one who never follows a truth through to its logical conclusion." It is not enough to look at a distant goal; we must find and do the concrete acts which will be the means of reaching the goal. One who leaves his mind behind when he enters the church and its life, and is content to be just "good hearted," may fail to see the anti-Christian nature of race hatred and prejudice; or the evils of a society dominated by greed; or the definite policies that lead to war.

Let us add another verse to that grand spiritual: "Lord, I want to be a Christian *in my mind*."

101 ✿ *The Saints Preserve Us!*

T HE WORDS above used to be heard frequently, and still are, in some places, as an ejaculation. In some ways, they make a polite and reverential form of swearing. When people are confronted with something they dislike heartily, or with something they fear, they exclaim: "The saints preserve us!" It is punctuated with an exclamation point.

We ought never to forget that those words make an affirmation as well as an ejaculation. They can mean not merely "May the saints preserve us," but also an accurate observation of history—"the saints *do preserve us*." Great souls, who have been called saints for their vision of God and His meaning for life, and their selfish dedication to Him and His work, do preserve the human race from spiritual blindness and destruction.

This is affirmed in the words of one of the saints, St. Paul, in his declaration: "The saints shall judge the world." Some who read those words may feel like exclaiming, "How ridiculous!" The saints *have* preserved the moral and spiritual standards by which the world is judged. And in time, in many things, the world has come to acknowledge the judgment of the saints. That was true on the judgment of Christian saints in gladiatorial contests in Rome, on slavery. By the grace of God, it will be true of war.

The saints do preserve us from blind self-satisfaction. They lift a standard for living to which men, in their deepest hearts, give assent. That was true of saints like St. Francis, John Bunyan, David Livingstone, Father Damien. They walk before our eyes, and in their presence our best reasserts itself. They make us ashamed of our mediocrity and bring us to repentance. *The New York Times* four years ago recorded the fact that a seventy-eight-year-old schoolteacher, Miss Harriet F. Hubbard, of Brooklyn, when she died, left her eyes to the Eye Bank for Sight, that they might be used for preserving sight for

180

someone living. The eyes were flown to Baltimore and the corneas transplanted. That is a picture of what the saints do for men. They have left the world, their "eyes," their vision of God's will, that the spiritual sight of humanity might be preserved.

The saints also preserved the *church*. The saints in any church are not people with stained-glass window perfection, but people separated from the compulsions of the world's standards and devoted to God's kingdom. These are the people who save the church from becoming chiefly a secular institution. They are in Jesus' words, the "salt of the earth" and of the church.

102 ❖ "So Easily Beset Us"

AN OLD TEXT, always in order. Never more in order, however, than when it is taken quite literally. Not sin, in general. Denouncing sin in general rarely bothers anyone. But the sins that do so easily beset *us*.

Emphasis on *us*! For instance, ask a typical middle-class congregation of fine people, fairly comfortable, what are the sins that do so easily beset *them*?

One thing will be clear immediately. There are many sins which do not really beset us at all. That does not mean that men and women in the congregation are saints, but simply that there are some directions in which their tastes do not run. The average members of our churches are not tempted to thieving, or murder, or drunkenness, or gross sexual immorality. Training and habit have very largely freed them from such sins. Dr. Henry Sloane Coffin once said in a sermon that a congregation would be shocked if their preacher said some morning: "I have a particular message for the thieves in the congregation."

Those are not our pitfalls.

What sins do, then, beset *us*?

With the usual middle-class congregation in mind, two sins may be stressed and watched for and prayed against.

One is *complacency*.

There is tremendous danger that a group of people who are pretty well off, who have escaped the grosser sins of the flesh, will become complacent over their own conditions, and over the ills and sufferings of others not of their particular group. We may get surrounded by a little wall of protection. The smug feeling, "we are not doing so badly," may prevent that repentance which is the necessary beginning of all true spiritual progress. A secure economic position may render

182

callous that sympathy and outgoing love which is a core of Christianity.

Another sin is *like-mindedness*.

A church which is made up largely of one class may get to take its dominant ideas from the accepted codes and ways of thinking of that class, and not from the thinking and words of Jesus. Too much like-mindedness may be a sort of mental and spiritual chloroform. If an idea is not the accepted thing in our circle, among people of our economic class, we may not even look at it. That happened among church people in England, when the condition of the child workers in mine and factory in the early nineteenth century was brought to their attention. The placing of the welfare of children before the divine right of dividends was not an "accepted" idea in middle-class circles. So it was with slavery. So with many ideas, embodying a truer justice. Like-mindedness in our group must give way to like-mindedness with Christ.

103 ✿ The Zero Hour

IN CLIFFORD DOWDEY'S book on the War Between the States, entitled *Experiment in Rebellion*, he has a strange passage which tells that during the Peninsular Campaign, when the Union Army under General McClelland was about twenty miles from Richmond and it looked as though the city would be captured, Jefferson Davis, President of the Confederate States, was baptized in his home by the rector of a neighboring church and received into the fellowship of the church.

Think of putting that off until the zero hour had arrived! All through his sixty years he had refused to line himself up with the Church of Christ. But when the Union Army was twenty miles away, he ran for cover!

Do not a great many people put off any real attention to religion until some time of crisis?

This last moment taking up of religion is too late. It is never too late for God to forgive sins, but it is too late for the Christian religion to have the effects in life which it might have. If we wait until some time of crisis, *we are too late to have religion as a guiding force during the whole of life.*

If we wait until some crisis comes upon us, *it is too late for faith, guiding us through the years, to build up support for the crisis itself.*

We cannot improvise a tree overnight, and we cannot improvise a faith overnight. There is nothing more pathetic than to see people try to pray in some crisis when they have not really prayed for twenty years.

When we come to Christianity only in a crisis, *it is too late to have one of its greatest joys—that of rendering a life of service,*

104 ❖ *Challenging an Axiom*

S OMEONE ONCE asked Albert Einstein: "How did it come about that you hit on the theory of relativity?"

He replied: "I challenged an axiom."

He looked at things which people had accepted without examination squarely in the face, and discovered they were not completely true. Progress has come partly because someone dared to challenge beliefs that were regarded as axiomatic.

Jesus did exactly that all his life. He said: "You have heard it said —but *I* say unto you. . . ." He challenged things which tradition never examined.

It is a good thing for Christians to look at our world and challenge some of the ideas that are accepted by millions of people in our time without any real examination.

Challenge the axiom that *success is the most important thing in the world*. Very few people say it in plain words. Millions live it in plain deeds. They act as though nothing else is important. Just look at the cost of success to all that is finest and most enduring in life, when success is made the main or only thing. The "axiom" will be found to be a pretentious lie.

Many people accept this as axiomatic—that *religion is a dull affair*. Not everyone, thank God. There are many whose lives prove that it can be the most lively and exhilarating affair that a person can engage in. Others accept the idea that religion is dull, and consequently are kept from discovering otherwise.

Millions accept as true the belief *that certain races or nationalities are superior*. There is no foundation for this in science. There is no foundation for it in the Christian gospel.

We hear over and over again the old proclamation *that armament races are the best means of preserving peace*. Against that moth-eaten falsehood, check the history of the world for the last twenty-five years. All armament races in history have ended in one place—the cemetery.

105 ✿ *Accessories Before the Fact*

A GOOD TEXT to go with the thoughts that follow is one from a book from which few sermons are ever preached: "In the day that thou stoodest on the other side . . . thou wast as one of them" (Obadiah 1:11).

The title above, "Accessories Before the Fact," comes from a law dealing with crime of many sorts. If a person helps bank robbers get away, he is guilty as an "accessory *after* the fact." If he helps to plan it and takes no part in it, or if he merely knows about its coming up and does not act on that knowledge, he is an "accessory *before* the fact."

With every great world tragedy there have been many "accessories *before* the fact." There have been many people who were responsible in the degree to which they might have done something to prevent it, and did nothing. Those who sit passively today and watch the possibility of World War III come nearer, and do nothing, are guilty of increasing that possibility.

We can see this more clearly if we look retrospectively at World War II. Stephen Spender pictures this vividly in his memoirs, *World within World*. He writes of the slaughtering of the Jews by Hitler before the war actually began:

Almost as terrible as the actions of the Nazis was the indifference of many people to these things, the lack of horror in the face of horror. This was more than a failure to read the signs of the approaching war. It was a moral indifference among those not directly involved, although just such callousness had made Fascism possible among the Germans. Certain Germans, living in some square of a German city, could be reproached for not inquiring into the disappearance of neighbors who were Jews or communists. But this attitude was equally reprehensible in people of other nations who allowed individuals and whole groups and finally even nations to be crushed.

187

They saw it and did nothing. They were guilty *before* the fact!

Now look in the other direction toward the future. How about it? Are we guilty of inaction against the forces that lead surely to war? What are some of them? Let the historian Arnold Toynbee tell us. In his six-volume study of history, he examines the fall of twenty-one civilizations before our own. He points out three marks of disintegration which preceded the death of every civilization which he studied. Here they are: First, a Messianic trust in military might; second, idolatry generally of the state; third, growing mechanization and specialization of common life.

Now look how those same three diseases are infecting our life as a nation: the budget of over thirty-four billion dollars a year for military might; a growing cult of worship of the state; and large mechanization of our common life.

Unless we oppose these trends, we become guilty *before* the awful fact of a third world war.

106 ❋ Extraordinary!

THERE IS a very arresting entry in the *Journal of Arnold Bennett*, the British novelist. When he had finished correcting the proofs of his novel, *Clayhanger*, he wrote in his *Journal*: "I notice the far too frequent use of the word 'extraordinary.' But I loathe altering a work once it is done."

We might say to Mr. Bennett that this was not so bad a failing after all. The opposite is far more common in life. The too frequent use of the word "ordinary" is a far worse fault. We have a fatal gift for making what is truly *extraordinary* seem only *ordinary*. The poet Wordsworth describes memorably the fading of the extraordinary into the very ordinary:

> The youth who daily farther from the east
> Must travel, still is Nature's priest,
> And by the vision splendid
> Is on his way attended,
> At length the man perceives it die away
> And fade into the light of common day.

It is always a very sad day when the vision of God fades away into the light of very ordinary day. But when there is a more frequent feeling for and use of the word "extraordinary" in our Christian faith and life, we get back into the experience and the spirit of the church depicted in the Book of Acts. The earliest Christian never ceased to be overcome by the sheer wonder of the gospel and the church.

Try this experiment. Go through the Acts and Epistles and note how many sentences need to be punctuated by exclamation points. Of course, in the New Testament manuscripts there were no exclamation points. These had to be supplied according to the sense. But how many exclamations of wonder there are. "Behold, what manner of love the Father hath bestowed upon us." "O the depth of the riches and wisdom and knowledge of God." There are many more.

189

The first-century Christians made very frequent use of the word "extraordinary" because the wonder of God's love never faded into the light of common day. The gospel was a breath-taking wonder. The church was extraordinary.

But how different it often is with us. We allow it to become ordinary from familiarity. Familiarity, that is, on the surface only. Think of the wonders we permit to fade. There is the supreme wonder that God should have stepped into our humanity in Christ!

There is the wonder of God's love for us as individuals, a wonder that is expressed truly though in colloquial language, in the old song, "I wonder as I wander," in which the singer is amazed that God should love a "poor ornery person like me." There was the amazement of the church, the body of Christ. Yet, very often, in the thought of many, it is a very "ordinary" organization, somewhat below their devotion to the lodge, the grange, or a dozen other groups!

How about your vocabulary? For the greatest mystery of the Christian gospel and faith is not that Jesus turned water into wine, but that he does turn what is often ordinary life into extraordinary experience and value.

107 ❀ "I Need the Church When..."

A PARAGRAPH which sometimes appears in church bulletins and orders of service raises questions worth thoughtful and vigorous thinking. It is the paragraph in which Edgar Guest, the popular versifier, tells of his need of the Church. Here it is:

To say that I do not need the Church is mere bravado. I needed it when my father died. I needed it when we were married. And when our babies were taken from us. I shall need it again, and need it badly.

We can be grateful for that declaration. And we may say: "Good." That is, good as far as it goes. But it does not go nearly far enough. It presents sharply just what is the matter with the idea of the Church held by multitudes of people, by very nominal Christians.

There is no discount to be made on Edgar Guest's sincerity. But as the words read, they stress the importance of the Church on two sorts of occasions only—formal, liturgical occasions, such as weddings and funerals, and on dark and gloomy days of sorrow.

We can thank God for help on both of these occasions. But think how much that statement of Mr. Guest's leaves out! It leaves out much of the whole genius of the Christian faith and revelation. This faith is not chiefly for the *end* of life, but for the beginning of life, when character is being formed and the springs of life are coiled, when goals are chosen, and when life is confronted with the call of Jesus: "Follow me." It is support for the heat of the day, when the down-pulling forces of the world are strong. It is needed not only when children are baptized or die, but when they need nurture and training. We need the Church to stir life with a great purpose, such as the struggle for a Christian order of life and a world-wide Church.